RUSSIA 1917–1939
GCSE Modern World History for Edexcel

Steve Waugh
John Wright

This material has been endorsed by Edexcel and offers high quality support for the delivery of Edexcel qualifications. Edexcel endorsement does not mean that this material is essential to achieve any Edexcel qualification, nor does it mean that this is the only suitable material available to support any Edexcel qualification. No endorsed material will be used verbatim in setting any Edexcel examination and any resource lists produced by Edexcel shall include this and other appropriate texts. While this material has been through an Edexcel quality assurance process, all responsibility for the content remains with the publisher. Copies of official specifications for all Edexcel qualifications may be found on the Edexcel website – www.edexcel.org.uk.

The Publishers would like to thank the following for permission to reproduce copyright material:

Photo credits
p. 6l © AKG Images; p. 6 r © Granger Collection/Topfoto; p. 7 © David King Collection; p. 9 © Getty/Hulton; p. 10, 11, 12 b © David King Collection; p. 12 t © Ria Novosti Photo Library; p. 13, 14, 15, 16 all, 19 b © David King Collection; p. 19 tr © CORBIS/Hulton-Deutsch; p. 21 © Getty/Hulton; p. 22, 23, 27 both © David King Collection; p. 29 © Getty Images; p. 30, 31, 33, 34 35 r © David King Collection; p. 36 © the Print Collector/HIP/Topfoto; p. 40, 43, 44 © David King Collection; p. 46 l © AKG Images; p. 46 r, 49, 53 © David King Collection; p. 54 © CORBIS/Hulton-Deutsch; p. 57 b © CORBIS; p. 59, 61, 63 r, 64, 65 © David King Collection; p. 67 © Getty-Hulton; p. 68, 70 both, 71 all, 73, 75 both, 76 b, 77 r, 78, 79, 80 © David King Collection; p. 82 Network/Alex Chusonov; p. 86, 87 t © David King Collection; p. 87 b © Topfoto; p. 88 © AKG Images; p. 89 © Marion Stratton Gould Fund, 2001.20.21, Memorial Art Gallery of the University of Rochester; p. 91 © AKG Images; p. 95 © Bettmann/CORBIS; p. 98, 99, 100 © David King Collection; p. 101 © Roger Perrin/The Bridgeman Art Library; p. 102 © Topfoto; p. 105, 106 t © David King Collection; p. 108, 109 b © Ria Novosti Photo Library; p. 110 both, 111, 112 © David King Collection; p. 117 © Bridgeman Art Library; p. 118 © Internationaal Instituut voor Sociale Geschiedenis, Amsterdam; p. 120 © AKG Images.

Examination practice artwork
p. 24, 39, 48, 60, 74, 84, 92, 93, 114 Stefan Chabluk

Acknowledgements
p. 5 Edexcel Limited, 2008 GCSE Modern World History paper, 2HA01 new specification booklet, p. 62; p. 59 r, J. Brooman, *Russia in War and Revolution*, Pearson Education Limited, 1986; p. 85 and 90 tl J. Brooman, *Stalin and the Soviet Union*, Pearson Education Limited, 1988; p. 67, 97 t and 121 T. Downey, *Russia and the USSR 1900–1995*, Oxford University Press, 1996; p. 37 D. Evans and J. Jenkins, *Years of Russia and the USSR 1851–1991*, Hodder Murray; p. 9, 14, 20 b, 21 r, 22, 24 both, 26 all, 45, 79 both, 88, 96 and 118 T. Fiehn, *Russia and the USSR*, Hodder Murray, 1996; p. 81 t E. Ginsburg, *Within the Whirlwind*, Harvest Press, 1982; p . 59 l, 97 b H. Hist and C. Baker, *Russia 1917–45*, Heinemann, 1990; p. 72 N. Kelly, *Russia and the USSR 1905–56*, Heinemann, 1996; p. 109 r Kravchenko, *I Chose Freedom*, 1946; p. 25 r, 65, 78 and 82 J. Laver, *Russia and the USSR 1905–56*, Hodder Murray, 1997; p. 29, 47 l, 66 and 94 M. Lynch, *Reaction and Revolution: Russia, 1894–1924*, Hodder Murray, 2005; p. 86 M. McCauley, *Stalin and Stalinism*, Pearson Education Limited, 1988; p. 81b F. MacLean, *Portrait of the Soviet Union*, Weidenfeld & Nicolson, 1988; p. 102 A. Nove, *An Economic History of the USSR*, Penguin, 1990; p. 12, 20 t, 32 and 44 b T. Pimlott, *Russian Revolution*, Macmillan, 1985; p. 44 tr R. Pipes, *The Russian Revolution*, Random House, Inc.; p. 53 r, 54, 55, 90 and 98 l R. Radway, *Russia and the USSR 1900–95*, Stanley Thorne Publishers, 1996; p. 13l, 17 both and 31, J. Robottom, *Russia in Change 1870–1945 Modern Times*, Pearson Education Limited, 1984; p. 44 tl and 62 V. Serge, Oxford University Press, 1967; p. 13 r and 21 l J. Shuter, *Russia and USSR 1905–56*, Heinemann, 1996; p. 15, 25 l, 38 t, 41, 51 both, 52 and 53 l J. Simkin, *The Russian Revolution*, Spartacus, 1986; p. 104 M. Sholokov, *Virgin Soil Upturned*, University Press of the Pacific, 2000; p. 80 A. Solzhenitsyn, *The Gulag Archipelago*, Harper Perennial, 2007; p. 111 l and 121 Freda Utley, *Lost Illusion*, George Allen & Unwin, 1949; p. 115 James von Geldern and Richard Stites (eds), *Mass Culture in Soviet Russia*, Indiana University Press, 1995, Reprinted with permission of Indiana University Press; p. 91 B. Walsh, *Modern World History*, Hodder Murray, 1996.

Every effort has been made to trace all copyright holders, but if any have been inadvertently overlooked the Publishers will be pleased to make the necessary arrangements at the first opportunity.

Although every effort has been made to ensure that website addresses are correct at time of going to press, Hodder Education cannot be held responsible for the content of any website mentioned in this book. It is sometimes possible to find a relocated web page by typing in the address of the home page for a website in the URL window of your browser.

Orders: please contact Bookpoint Ltd, 130 Milton Park, Abingdon, Oxon OX14 4SB. Telephone: (44) 01235 827720. Fax: (44) 01235 400454. Lines are open 9.00 – 5.00, Monday to Saturday, with a 24-hour message answering service. Visit our website at www.hoddereducation.co.uk.

© John Wright, Steve Waugh 2006, 2009
First published in 2006 by
Hodder Education,
An Hachette UK Company
338 Euston Road
London NW1 3BH

Edited and produced for Hodder Education by White-Thomson Publishing/Kelly Davis/www.wtpub.co.uk
Telephone: 0845 362 8240.

This second edition published 2009

Impression number   5 4 3 2 1
Year   2013 2012 2011 2010 2009

All rights reserved. Apart from any use permitted under UK copyright law, no part of this publication may be reproduced or transmitted in any form or by any means, electronic or mechanical, including photocopying and recording, or held within any information storage and retrieval system, without permission in writing from the publisher or under licence from the Copyright Licensing Agency Limited. Further details of such licences (for reprographic reproduction) may be obtained from the Copyright Licensing Agency Limited, Saffron House, 6-10 Kirby Street, London EC1N 8TS.

Cover photos © Musée de l'Armée, Brussels, Belgium, Patrick Lorette/The Bridgeman Art Libraray; © Buyenlarge/Time Life Pictures/Getty Images.
Typeset in Adobe Garamond 12 pt by White-Thomson Publishing Ltd
Printed in Italy

A catalogue record for this title is available from the British Library.

ISBN: 978 0340 984 406

Contents

Introduction	4
Key Topic 1: The collapse of the tsarist regime, 1917	**6**
Chapter 1 The nature of tsarist rule at the beginning of 1917	7
Chapter 2 The impact of the First World War	17
Chapter 3 The fall of the tsar and the establishment of the Provisional Government	25
Key Topic 2: Bolshevik takeover and consolidation, 1917–24	**40**
Chapter 4 The October Revolution	41
Chapter 5 Imposing Bolshevik control, 1917–21	49
Chapter 6 Creating a new society, 1918–24	61
Key Topic 3: The nature of Stalin's dictatorship, 1924–39	**68**
Chapter 7 The struggle for power, 1924–28	69
Chapter 8 The purges of the 1930s	75
Chapter 9 Propaganda and censorship	85
Key Topic 4: Economic and social changes, 1928–39	**94**
Chapter 10 Collectivisation	95
Chapter 11 Industrialisation	105
Chapter 12 Life in the Soviet Union	115
Revision activities	122
Glossary	125
Index	127

Introduction

About the course
During this course you must study four units:

- **Unit 1** Peace and War: International Relations 1900–1991
- **Unit 2** Modern World Depth Study
- **Unit 3** Modern World Source Enquiry
- **Unit 4** Representations of History.

These units are assessed through three examination papers and one controlled assessment:

- In Paper 1 you have one hour and 15 minutes to answer questions on three different topics from Unit 1 (International Relations 1900–1991).
- In Paper 2 you have one hour and 15 minutes to answer questions on a Modern World Depth Study (Unit 2).
- In Paper 3 you have one hour and 15 minutes to answer source questions on one Modern World Source Enquiry topic (Unit 3).
- In the controlled assessment you have to complete a task under controlled conditions in the classroom (Unit 4).

Modern World Depth Study (Unit 2)
There are three options in the Modern World Depth Study unit. You have to study one. The three options are:

- **Option 2a:** Germany 1918–39
- **Option 2b:** Russia 1917–39
- **Option 2c:** The USA 1919–41

About the book
This book covers the main developments in Russia from 1917 to 1939. The book is divided into four key topics, each with three chapters:

- **Key Topic 1** examines the collapse of the tsarist regime, including the nature of tsarist rule, the impact of the First World War and the fall of the tsar in 1917.
- **Key Topic 2** explains the Bolshevik takeover and consolidation of power 1917–24, including the October Revolution, how Bolshevik control was imposed in the years 1917–21 and the creation of a new society, 1918–1924.
- **Key Topic 3** concentrates on the nature of Stalin's dictatorship in the years 1924–39, including the struggle for power from 1924 to 1928, the purges of the 1930s and the use of propaganda and censorship.
- **Key Topic 4** examines the economic and social changes between 1928 and 1939, including industrialisation, collectivisation and life in the Soviet Union.

Each chapter in this book:

- Contains activities – some develop the historical skills you will need, others are exam-style questions that give you the opportunity to practise exam skills. The exam-style questions are highlighted in blue.
- Gives step-by-step guidance, model answers and advice on how to answer particular question types in Unit 2.
- Defines key terms and highlights glossary terms in bold the first time they appear in each key topic.

About Unit 2
Unit 2 is a test of:

- Knowledge and understanding of the key developments in Russia 1917–39
- The ability to answer brief and extended essay-type questions and a source inference question.

You have to answer the following types of questions. Each requires you to demonstrate different historical skills:

- **Inference** – getting messages from a source
- **Causation** – explaining why something happened
- **Consequence** – explaining the effects or results of an event
- **Change** – explaining how and why changes occurred
- **Describe** – giving a detailed description, usually of the key events in a given period. This is also known as the key features question
- **Judgement** – assessing the importance of causes, changes or consequences. This is also known as the scaffolding question.

Below is a set of specimen questions (without the sources). You will be given step-by-step guidance throughout the book on how best to approach and answer these types of questions.

> This is a **source inference** question. You have to get a message or messages from the source.

> This is a **describe** question. You have to describe the key features of historical actions or events.

> This is a **consequence** question. You have to explain the effects or results of an event.

> This is a **causation** question. You have to explain why something happened.

> This is a **change** or **'explain how'** question. You have to explain how or why something happened.

UNIT 2   EXAM

1 (a) What can you learn from Source A about the problems facing Tsar Nicholas II in 1917?

(4 marks)

1 (b) Describe the key features of the government of Russia under Tsar Nicholas II before the revolution in February 1917.

(6 marks)

1 (c) Explain the effects of the February Revolution on Russia in 1917.

(8 marks)

1 (d) Explain why the Bolsheviks were able to seize power in October 1917.

(8 marks)

2 Explain how Stalin was able to overcome his leadership rivals in the years 1924–28.

(8 marks)

3 Was the Stakhanovite movement the main reason for the rapid expansion of Soviet industry in the 1930s? Explain your answer.
You may use the following information to help you with your answer.
- The Stakhanovite movement
- Gosplan
- The First Five-Year Plan
- Role of women

(16 marks)

> This is a **scaffolding** question, which gives you four main points. You should develop at least three clear points and judge and explain the importance of each.

(Total 50 marks)

Introduction   5

Key Topic 1: The collapse of the tsarist regime, 1917

Source A: A painting of the coronation of Tsar Nicholas. It was completed in 1898, two years after the coronation

Source B: A photograph of Russian peasants in about 1900

Task
What can you learn about Russia in the early twentieth century from Sources A and B?

This key topic examines the turbulent history of Russia from the beginning of the twentieth century to the fall of Tsar Nicholas II in 1917. This was a remarkable period which saw the tsar hold on to his power after a revolution in 1905 but then lose it some twelve years later at the height of the First World War. These first three chapters examine how the seemingly unchallengeable tsar surrendered his throne rather meekly in February 1917.

Each chapter explains a key issue and examines important lines of enquiry as outlined below:

Chapter 1 The nature of tsarist rule at the beginning of 1917 (pages 7–16)

- How was Russia ruled?
- Why was Nicholas II such a weak tsar?
- Why was the Russian economy so backward in the early twentieth century?
- Why were the peasants and town workers discontented?
- Why was there growth of opposition to Nicholas II?
- Which political groups opposed the tsar?

Chapter 2 The impact of the First World War on Russia (pages 17–24)

- What was Russia's involvement in the First World War?
- Why did Russia suffer so many defeats?
- What effects did these defeats have?
- What were the effects of the war?

Chapter 3 The fall of the tsar and the establishment of the Provisional Government (pages 25–39)

- Why was there a revolution in Russia in February 1917?
- What were the weaknesses and failures of the Provisional Government?
- What was the significance of the Kornilov Revolt?

1 The nature of tsarist rule at the beginning of 1917

Tasks

Study Source A.

1. Each numbered arrow represents a different class or group in Russian society. Try to identify each one.

2. What message is the cartoonist trying to put across about Russian society in the early twentieth century?

Source A: Cartoon showing the different groups in Russia in the early twentieth century

Russia at the beginning of the twentieth century was a vast empire covering one-sixth of the world's surface. It was ruled by Tsar Nicholas II, who faced a number of political, economic, social, religious and geographical problems.

This chapter will answer the following questions:

- How was Russia ruled?
- Why was Nicholas II such a weak tsar?
- Why was the Russian economy so backward in the early twentieth century?
- Why were the peasants and town workers discontented?
- Why was there growth of opposition to Nicholas II?
- Which political groups opposed the tsar?

How was Russia ruled?

The Russian Empire in the early twentieth century

Geographical problems

The map above shows some of the reasons why the size of the Russian Empire made it difficult to govern. It was also difficult to rule because of the many different peoples or ethnic groups in the empire. The total population of 125 million was made up of more than 20 different peoples. For six people out of every ten, Russian was a foreign language.

Many of these peoples resented being part of the empire, especially as the rulers of Russia carried out a policy of Russification. This meant making non-Russians speak Russian, wear Russian clothes and follow Russian customs. For example, in the area of present-day Poland, it was forbidden to teach children in Polish. Russians were often given the important jobs in non-Russian areas.

Tasks

1. Using the map, suggest reasons why the size of the Russian Empire made it so difficult to govern.

2. Why do you think the many non-Russian groups in the Russian Empire were known as the 'subject' nationalities?

3. What was meant by 'Russification'? Start by defining the term and then give examples of how it was carried out.

How did the tsar govern Russia?

Russia was an **autocracy** with all the power in the hands of the tsar. The tsar believed that he had a divine right to rule – that is, he had been chosen by God. This meant he could do whatever he liked without having to consult his people. There was no parliament to represent the people's views.

The tsar did have a council of ministers that ran the various government departments, but they could not make important decisions. There were thousands of civil servants, such as tax collectors, who carried out the day-to-day work of government. They were generally poorly paid, so this encouraged bribery and corruption.

The Russian people had little freedom. All unions of workers and strikes were forbidden, and newspapers and books were censored by the government. The tsar was determined to suppress all opposition through the *Okhrana*, his secret police. They used spies and agents to root out anyone who was against the tsar and his system of government. Such opponents could be imprisoned without trial or exiled to far-off Siberia.

> **Source A:** Extract from a letter from Tolstoy, a Russian novelist, who wrote to Tsar Nicholas II about the discontent at the time
>
> A third of the whole of Russia lives under police surveillance. The army of the police, both regular and secret, is continually growing in numbers. The prisons are overcrowded with thousands of convicts and political prisoners. **Censorship** has reached its highest level since the 1840s. In all cities ... soldiers are ... equipped with live ammunition to be sent out against the people.

The Orthodox Church

About 70 per cent of the population were members of the official **Orthodox Church**. The Church was very closely linked to the tsar and supported his way of ruling. It taught that the tsar was the head of the country and the Church – in other words, that he was God's chosen representative on earth.

It was unpopular because large minorities belonged to other Churches and religions, and resented the power and privileges of the Orthodox Church. For example, nine per cent were Roman Catholic and eleven per cent Muslim. Also, the Church was very wealthy, which contrasted greatly to the poor lifestyle of the majority of Russian people.

> **Source B:** A late nineteenth-century painting of a religious procession inside a Russian Orthodox Church

> ### Tasks
>
> 4. What does Source A show about how Russia was ruled in the early twentieth century?
>
> 5. Why do you think Tolstoy wrote an open letter to the tsar? What was he hoping to achieve?
>
> 6. Source A gives only an extract from Tolstoy's letter. Using information from this section, add another paragraph to his letter about other reasons for discontent in Russia.
>
> 7. What does Source B show you about the Orthodox Church? Does it support any of the reasons about why it was unpopular?

Chapter 1 The nature of tsarist rule at the beginning of 1917

Why was Nicholas II such a weak tsar?

The system of autocracy only worked if the tsar was strong and able to control the government and different nationalities of the vast Russian Empire. Nicholas II, who became tsar in 1894, was not a strong character. He was reluctant to become tsar, possibly because he witnessed the assassination of his grandfather, Alexander II, in 1881. When Nicholas became tsar in 1894 he said:

> 'What is going to happen to me? I am not prepared to be Tsar. I never wanted to become one. I know nothing of the business of ruling. I have no idea of even how to talk to ministers.'

Nicholas II insisted on governing as an autocrat. He and his wife, the Tsarina Alexandra, believed that they had been chosen by God to rule and that no one had the right to challenge them. He was ignorant of the nature and extent of opposition to tsarist rule and refused to share power. It was once said that 'The two most important people in Russia are Tsar Nicholas II and the last person to whom he had spoken'.

Although a devoted husband and father, he was not particularly happy. His only son and heir, Alexis, suffered from an incurable blood disease known as **haemophilia** and was likely to die young.

Source A: Extract from the diary of the tsar's sister, the Grand Duchess Olga

'He had intelligence, . . . faith and courage but he was . . . ignorant about governmental matters. Nicky had been trained as a soldier. He had not been taught statesmanship and . . . was not a statesman.'

Source B: Nicholas II and his family

Tasks

1. In what ways does Source B support the evidence of Source A about Nicholas II? Explain your answer.

2. How would Nicholas have responded to Tolstoy's open letter on page 9? Write a letter of reply to Tolstoy from the tsar. Remember that he believed in the system of autocracy and the need to suppress opposition, especially after the assassination of his grandfather.

3. What was meant when it was said that the 'second most important person in Russia was the last person to whom Nicholas II had spoken'?

Why was the Russian economy so backward in the early twentieth century?

Most of the population, 85 per cent, lived in the countryside. Russian agriculture, however, was poor. Extensive tundra, forest and desert meant only about five per cent of the land, mainly in the south-west, was used for farming (see map, page 8). Old-fashioned farming methods resulted in low food production and frequent famines. In most villages the land was divided into three large fields.

> **Source A:** A photograph taken in 1892 showing starving peasants being given food during a famine

Each household had strips in each of these fields. This scattered strip farming system encouraged subsistence farming using primitive hand tools.

Even though Russia was rich in oil and minerals, industrialisation did not happen until the end of the nineteenth century (much later than some other European countries, such as Britain and Germany). Considering Russia's size and resources, its manufacturing output was still very low at the beginning of the twentieth century. Its size and undeveloped system of roads and railways, together with the absence of an effective banking system, all restricted the growth of industry.

By the outbreak of the First World War, Russia had experienced a rapid growth in industry due to:
- an increase in the output of coal in the Ukraine
- an increase in the output of oil in the Caucasus
- deliberate government policy.

One of the tsar's ministers, Count Sergei Witte, who was minister of finance from 1893 to 1903, set himself the huge task of modernising the Russian economy. He invited foreign experts and workers to advise on industrial planning and techniques. His reforms did stimulate industrial growth, as can be seen in the table below.

Russia also experienced the social problems that normally go with early and rapid industrialisation. Many peasants moved to the towns and cities to work in industry. This brought problems with living and working conditions.

	Annual production (in millions of tonnes)			
	Coal	Pig iron	Oil	Grain*
1880	3.2	0.42	0.5	34
1890	5.9	0.89	3.9	36
1900	16.1	2.66	10.2	56
1910	26.8	2.99	9.4	74
1913	35.4	4.12	9.1	90
1916	33.8	3.72	9.7	64

(*European Russia only)

Russia's annual industrial production from 1880 to 1913

Tasks

1. What does Source A tell you about life in the Russian countryside?

2. Suggest two improvements to the normal farming practices that could have made it more efficient. Think about the strip farming system and the tools.

3. Examine the table of industrial production above. Why do you think grain production increased so much in this period? (One clue is Stolypin – see page 14.)

4. What were the key features of Russian industrial development in the late nineteenth and early twentieth centuries?

Why were the peasants and town workers discontented?

The Russian Empire was a land of great contrasts. As you have seen in Source A on page 7, Russian society was divided into various classes or groups. The vast majority of the people were poor peasants. At the other end of the scale, at the top, was the aristocracy.

> **Source A:** A typical flat for workers in the late 1890s

> **Source B:** A dinner party in the palace of Countess Yelisaveta Shuvalova in St Petersburg in 1900

What was life like for the wealthy?

The aristocracy made up just over one per cent of the population and yet they owned almost one-quarter of all the land. Some were extremely rich, with lavish homes in the countryside, a second home in a town or city and many servants.

> **Source C:** Tolstoy describes the lifestyle of a Russian nobleman, Prince Dmitri Ivanovich Nechlyudov
>
> *The prince proceeded to a long dining table where three servants had polished for a whole day. The room was furnished with a huge oak sideboard and an equally large table, the legs of which were carved in the shape of a lion's paws. On this table, which was covered with a fine starched cloth with large monograms, stood a coffee pot, a silver sugar bowl, a cream jug with hot cream, and a bread basket filled with freshly baked rolls.*

By 1914, Russia had a middle class whose numbers were increasing due to the development of industry. This included bankers, merchants and factory owners. Many made fortunes from government contracts and loans and had a very pleasant lifestyle, eating out at expensive restaurants and frequently going to the theatre or ballet.

The peasants

The biggest, and possibly poorest group, were the peasants. They made up nearly four out of every five Russian people in the years before 1917. For most, life was very hard. They lived in very poor conditions and survived on a staple diet of rye bread, porridge and cabbage soup. When the harvests were poor, there was starvation and disease. They had a life expectancy of less than 40 years, with many dying from typhus and diphtheria.

Many peasants felt bitter towards the nobles or aristocracy and their generally extravagant lifestyle. The nobles had kept most of the land when **serfdom** ended in 1861 and peasants resented having to work on nobles' estates to earn money.

A population growth of 50 per cent between 1860 and 1897 brought greater competition for land and even smaller peasant plots.

> **Source D:** A photograph of a starving peasant family

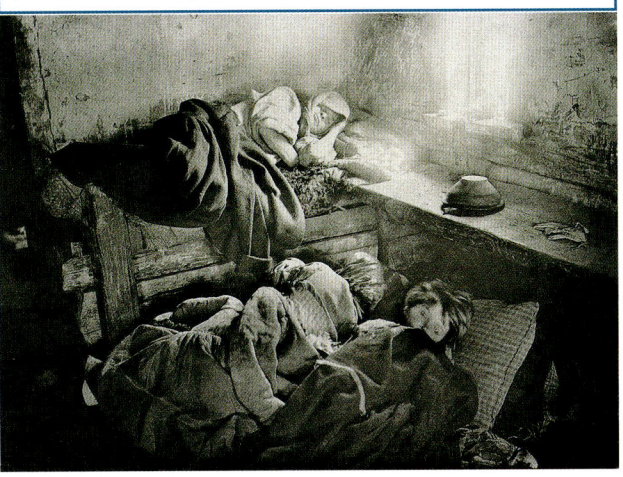

> **Source E:** A Russian lady, who led a relief party that took food to the Volga region suffering from famine in 1892, describes what she witnessed
>
> *It was tragedy to see splendid men in the prime of their life walking about with stony faces and hollow eyes. And then there were women clothed only in wretched rags, and little children shivering in the cold wind. There were many of them who had not tasted food for days. It was agonising to hear these people pleading to us for mercy lest they die of starvation. There was no complaint, no cries, just the slow monotonous chant, broken by the sobs of worn out mothers and the cries of hungry children.*

The town workers

The final and most rapidly increasing group were the new workers in industry in the towns and cities. Large numbers of peasants had flocked to the towns and cities to work in industry. Their conditions were terrible. Workers lived in overcrowded slums and ate cheap black bread, cabbage soup and wheat porridge. In industrial centres away from the cities, workers often lived in barracks next to the factory and slept in filthy, overcrowded dormitories. They earned low wages, worked long hours and were forbidden to form trade unions to fight for better conditions. Protests or strikes were crushed, often with great brutality by the police or army.

> **Source F:** From *The Story of My Life*, by Father Gapon, written in 1905. Gapon was a priest who organised a trade union to help workers
>
> *They receive terrible wages, and generally live in overcrowded conditions. The normal working day is eleven and a half hours not including meal times. But manufacturers have received permission to use overtime. This makes the average day longer than that allowed by the law – fifteen or sixteen hours.*

Tasks

1. Look again at the cartoon showing the different groups in Russian society (Source A, page 7).

   a) Do your own sketch to show these different groups.
   b) Annotate your sketch with key words to show the main features of each group.

2. What do Sources A, B and C show you about the lifestyle of people in Russia at the beginning of the twentieth century? Explain your answer.

3. Make a copy of the following table and use the sources and information on these two pages and page 11 to complete it.

   - In the second column give a brief explanation for their discontent.
   - In the third column explain what you think the tsar should do to reduce or remove this discontent.

	Why discontented?	What tsar should do
Subject nationalities		
Peasants		
Town workers		

Chapter 1 The nature of tsarist rule at the beginning of 1917

Why was there growth of opposition to Tsar Nicholas II?

In the years before 1917, there was increasing opposition to Nicholas II for several reasons.

Reasons for the growth of opposition to Nicholas II

'Bloody Sunday', 22 January 1905

This was a peaceful march by around 200,000 people to the tsar's Winter Palace, led by Father Gapon, to petition for better working conditions. However, the tsar was not in his palace and the soldiers panicked. They fired on the crowd, killing hundreds and wounding thousands.

Source A: From a letter by an American diplomat in the Russian city of Odessa. He was writing about the consequences of Bloody Sunday

Tsar Nicholas has lost absolutely the affection of the Russian people, and whatever the future may have in store for the Romanovs, Nicholas will never again be safe in the midst of his people.

The 1905 Revolution

Bloody Sunday, together with the defeat of Russia in war with Japan (1904–05), sparked revolution in Russia. There were strikes and a mutiny in the navy. In order to avoid further chaos, Nicholas II issued the October Manifesto, which promised freedom of speech, an end to censorship and a national parliament (*duma*). This revolution was a warning to the tsar about the need for change and reform. However, Nicholas II ignored this warning.

Stolypin's 'necktie'

After the 1905 Revolution, Nicholas appointed Peter Stolypin as prime minister. Stolypin did introduce certain reforms, especially of agriculture and education. However, those who openly opposed the tsar were dealt with severely. There were more than 3000 executions during Stolypin's time as prime minister – and the gallows became known as 'Stolypin's necktie'.

The failure of the *dumas*

In the years after 1905 Nicholas ensured that the *duma* he had been forced to create had little power. After the election of the first *duma* in 1906, he declared that he had the power to dissolve it, and to change the rules by which it was elected, whenever he liked. There were four different *dumas* in the years 1906–14. Nicholas had gone against the promises made in his October Manifesto, refusing to share power and continuing to rule like an autocrat. This, in turn, stimulated further opposition.

Industrial unrest

As we have seen, Russia's rapid industrial growth had created poor living and working conditions for the industrial workers. This led to a wave of strikes in the years before 1914. One of the most important strikes occurred in 1912 at the Lena goldfields, where troops shot dead more than 200 strikers and injured several hundred. The events at Lena heralded a new wave of strikes in urban areas across Russia and there was a general strike in St Petersburg in July 1914.

Source B: Photograph showing some of the dead strikers at the Lena goldfields, 1912

Key Topic 1 The collapse of the tsarist regime, 1917

Rasputin

After 1907, Nicholas and his wife, Alexandra, came to rely on the help and guidance of a holy man named Gregory Rasputin. Rasputin had the ability to control the life-threatening illness of the tsar's son – Alexei suffered from **haemophilia**.

Alexandra and Nicholas called Rasputin 'Our Friend' and his position and power at court grew so much that he eventually helped to choose government ministers. Stories about his **hedonistic** lifestyle abounded, such as rumours of orgies, and there were always large numbers of women in his presence.

Rasputin was another piece of ammunition for those who did not like tsarism. These critics saw corruption and incompetence now being added to the list of problems that Russia faced.

> **Source C:** From a statement by Rodzianko, Octobrist politician, March 1916, about the evil influence of Rasputin
>
> I said to the Tsar – 'This cannot continue much longer. No one opens your eyes to the true role which Rasputin is playing. His presence in Your Majesty's Court undermines confidence in your Supreme Power and may have an evil effect …'
> My report did some good – Rasputin was sent away to Tobolsk, but a few days later, at the demand of the Empress, this order was cancelled.

Source D: One of the many postcards that circulated around St Petersburg in 1916 and 1917, showing Rasputin and Alexandra

Tasks

1. What does Source A suggest about the importance of 'Bloody Sunday'?

2. Devise a caption for Source B that could have been used by opponents of the tsar.

3. Why was Source D damaging for the supporters of the tsar?

4. Study Sources C and D. In what ways does Source D support the evidence of Source C about the influence of Rasputin? Explain your answer.

5. Copy the table below and then fill in the columns to show how opposition to the tsar was developing in the years before 1917.

Political issues	Economic issues	Social issues

Which political groups opposed the tsar?

The Social Democratic Party founded in 1901

Vladimir Lenin

The party followed the teachings of Karl Marx and believed that the workers (**proletariat**) would one day stage a revolution and remove the tsar. The revolution would lead to the setting up of a communist state. In 1903, the party split into two – **Mensheviks** and **Bolsheviks**. The Mensheviks believed that the party should have a mass membership and were prepared for slow change. The Bolsheviks believed that a small party **elite** should organise the revolution. Vladimir Lenin led the Bolsheviks and the Mensheviks were led by Julius Martov and Leon Trotsky.

The Socialist Revolutionaries (SRs) founded in 1901

Alexander Kerensky

The SRs, as they were called, believed in a revolution of the peasants and aimed to get rid of the tsar. They wanted to share all land among the peasants, so that it could be farmed in small peasant communities. There was a mixture of beliefs within the party – some wanted to use terror to achieve their aims and others were prepared to use constitutional methods. Terrorist activity by SR members led to the deaths of thousands of government officials in the years before 1917. Alexander Kerensky eventually led the SRs.

The Constitutional Democratic Party (Cadets) founded in 1905

Paul Milyukov

As Russia developed a middle class, the demand grew for a democratic style of government. The Cadets wanted to have a constitutional monarch and an elected parliament – as in Britain – though some were prepared to set up a republic. The Cadets were led by Paul Milyukov.

The Octobrists founded in October 1905

Alexander Guchkov

This party was set up after the tsar issued his October Manifesto. Its followers believed that the tsar would carry out his manifesto promises of limited reform. The Octobrists' main area of support came from the middle classes. It was led by Alexander Guchkov.

Tasks

1. Which of the political parties might Tsar Nicholas have feared the most? Explain your answer.
2. Working in pairs, devise a catchy political slogan for each of the four parties.

2 The impact of the First World War

Source A: An extract from the diary of Meriel Buchanan, the daughter of the British Ambassador to Russia. She describes reactions to Russian entry into the First World War

5 August 1914
The processions in the streets were carrying the Emperor's portrait with the bands playing the National Anthem. Women and girls flocked to work in the hospitals. Everywhere there is enthusiasm for the war. People are convinced that we are fighting in a just and holy war for the freedom and betterment of the world. We dream of triumph and victory. The war will be over by Christmas.

Source B: An extract from Meriel Buchanan's diary

December 1914
Grey days of biting cold, the silence of the snow hushing the bustling activity of the city to a sudden, almost disconcerting quiet. No balls, no music. The men we have danced with have lost their lives in East Prussia or were fighting in the Carpathians, the women were working in the hospitals, in field ambulances, in Red Cross trains. War! We now know the meaning of it in all its bitter and cruel truth. There are no cheering crowds, no flags carried round in procession and no bands playing the National Anthem.

Tasks

1. What does Source A suggest about attitudes in Russia to the war?
2. Does Source B support the evidence of Source A about attitudes to the war?

Russia entered the First World War with great expectations of success. Many believed the sheer size of the Russian armies, known as 'the Russian steamroller', would be too strong for both Germany and Austria–Hungary. However, by the end of 1916, Russia had suffered defeat after defeat and there was growing discontent with the tsar and his government.

This chapter will answer the following questions:

- What was Russia's involvement in the First World War?
- Why did Russia suffer so many defeats?
- What effects did these defeats have?
- What were the effects of the war?

Examination skills

This chapter gives guidance on question 1a from Unit 2. This question, which is worth four marks, is a source inference question.

What was Russia's involvement in the First World War?

When the heir to the Austrian throne, the Archduke Franz Ferdinand, was assassinated in Serbia on 28 June 1914, Austria, supported by Germany, declared war on the Serbs. Russia was the **protector** of Serbia, so the first reason Russia joined the war in August 1914 was to help Serbia.

Secondly, Russia also went to war to support France and Britain. All three countries were members of the **Triple Entente**.

What were the key military events of the war on the Eastern Front, 1914–16?

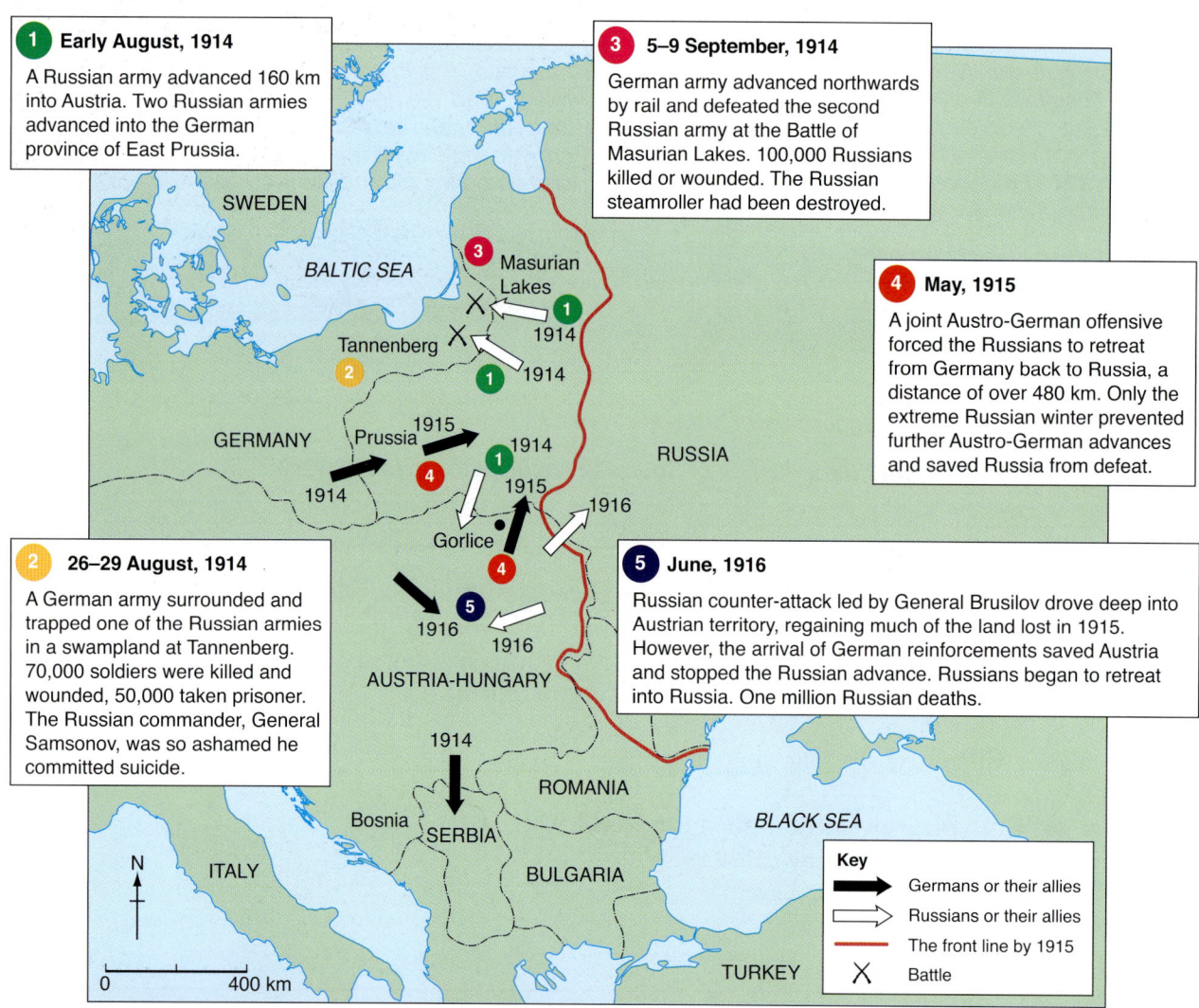

The key events on the Eastern Front, 1914–16

Key Topic 1 The collapse of the tsarist regime, 1917

DATE	EVENT
1914	
August	Russians advance into Austria and Germany
26–9 August	Battle of Tannenberg
5–9 September	Battle of Masurian Lakes
	By the end of 1914 Russia had over 1 million casualties
1915	
May	Austro-German offensive
August	Nicholas takes command of the Russian armies
	By the end of 1915 Germany and Austria-Hungary had control of 13 per cent of the Russian population including 16 million people
1916	
June	Brusilov offensive
Winter	All gains from Brusilov offensive lost

Timeline of events on the Eastern Front, 1914–16

Source B: The German general, von Moltke, describes the slaughter at Tannenberg

The sight of thousands of Russians driven into huge lakes and swamps was ghastly. The shrieks and cries of the dying men I will never forget. So fearful was the sight of these thousands of men with their guns, horses and ammunition, struggling in the water that, to shorten their agony, they turned the machine-guns on them. But even in spite of that, there was movement seen among them for a week after.

Source C: Germans guarding a pile of Russian corpses

Source A: A photograph showing Russian soldiers taken prisoner after the Battle of Tannenberg

Tasks

1. What does Source B suggest about the battle of Tannenberg?
2. In what ways does Source B support the evidence of Sources A and C? Explain your answer.

Chapter 2 The impact of the First World War

Why did Russia suffer so many defeats?

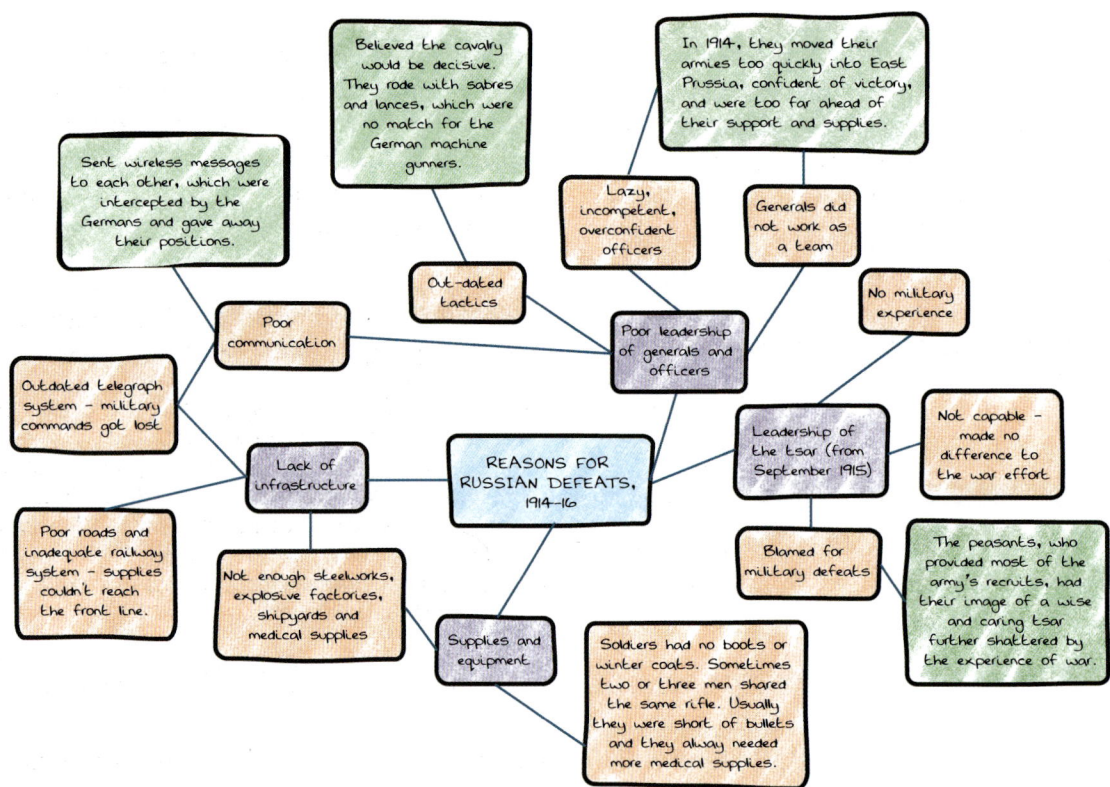

Tasks

1. Examine the concept map above, which shows the key reasons for Russia's defeats.
   - Explain how the different reasons are linked.
   - Rank the reasons in order of importance in the defeat of Russia.
   - Which do you think was the most important reason for the defeats? Explain why.

2. Why did Russia suffer so many defeats in the years 1914–16?

3. You are an adviser to Nicholas II who has been sent to the Eastern Front in September 1915. Write a memorandum to the tsar explaining the problems at the front and what needs to be done. Use Sources A and B and the concept map to help you.

Source A: From a letter written by the tsar to his wife in July 1916

Without metal the mills cannot supply a sufficient number of bullets and bombs. The same is true as regards the railways. The Minister of Transportation assures me that the railways are working better this year than last, but nevertheless every one complains that they are not doing as well as they might.

Source B: Written by Belaiev, a Russian general

In recent battles, a third of the men had no rifles. The poor devils had to wait patiently until their comrades fell before their eyes and they could pick up weapons. The army is drowning in its own blood.

Key Topic 1 The collapse of the tsarist regime, 1917

What effects did these defeats have?

Enthusiasm for the war soon waned. Casualties, frequent defeats and poor equipment lowered the morale of the soldiers. They soon lost respect for their officers, who seemed unfeeling and ineffective. Many soldiers died without weapons or ammunition, and some did not even have boots to wear in the bitterly cold weather.

This discontent spread to the people of Russia. News of high casualties caused alarm in different parts of the Russian Empire. For example, in Baku, the capital of Azerbaijan, women lay on the rails to stop troop trains moving. In other areas there was violent resistance to conscription.

Source A: A police report on army morale, October 1916

The behaviour of the soldiers, especially in the units in the rear, is most provocative. They accuse the military authorities of corruption, cowardice and drunkenness, and even treason. Everywhere one meets thousands of deserters, carrying out crimes and offering violence to the civilian population.

Source B: From a report by the Chairman of the Military Commission of the *duma*

As early as the beginning of the second year of the war, desertions of soldiers at the front and on their way to the front became commonplace, and the average number of deserters reached 25 per cent. I happen to know of three cases when the train was stopped because there were no passengers on it; all, with the exception of the officer in command, had run away.

Tasks

1. What does Source A suggest about the behaviour of some Russian soldiers?

2. Does Source B support the evidence of Source A about the behaviour of some Russian soldiers?

3. Study Source C. This photograph was probably taken by opponents of the tsar and the war. Devise a caption that they could have used with this photograph.

Source C: A photograph showing Russian deserters, including officers, in December 1916

Chapter 2 The impact of the First World War

What were the effects of the war?

Economic and social effects

The war had a devastating effect on the Russian economy. Inflation increased – there were seven price rises between 1913 and 1917. Less food was produced because of the shortage of labour and horses. As more peasants were called up to the armed forces, there were fewer men left to work on the land. Indeed, 14 million men were called up to serve in the army between 1914 and 1917. The demand for horses at the front also made it harder for peasants to cultivate their land. This, in turn, encouraged higher food prices.

Industry, too, was hit by the shortage of workers and by the lack of fuel and essential supplies. Russia's transport system could not cope with the increased demands of war, as well as providing industry with the necessary raw materials. Consumer goods, such as boots and cloth, became scarce and expensive. There were shortages of vital coal, iron and steel. Many factories closed, making their workers unemployed.

The economic problems brought misery. Because of the shortages, the prices were rising continually, but wages were hardly going up at all. To make matters worse, workers were being asked to work longer hours. The closure of factories led to unemployment and even greater poverty.

All these hardships were, in turn, worsened by fuel and food shortages. Even when fuel and food were available, supplies frequently failed to reach the people in the towns and cities, due to Russia's inadequate transport system and the incompetence of the government.

What was the situation at the beginning of 1917?

By the beginning of 1917, Russia was close to defeat on the Eastern Front and there was mass discontent in the armed forces and among the Russian people. To make matters worse, Petrograd experienced the worst winter in living memory, with temperatures falling below minus 30 degrees centigrade, at a time when there were severe food and fuel shortages.

Source A: A photograph showing people queuing for bread in Petrograd in early 1917

Source B: Police report from the end of 1916

The industrial proletariat of the capital is on the verge of despair. The smallest outbreak will lead to uncontrollable riots. Even if we assume that wages have increased by 100 per cent, the cost of living has risen by 300 per cent. The impossibility of obtaining food, the time wasted in queues outside shops, the increasing death rate due to inadequate diet and the cold and dampness as a result of the lack of coal and firewood – all these conditions have created such a situation that the mass of industrial workers are quite ready to let themselves go to the wildest excesses of a hunger riot.

Political effects

At first, the war seemed to improve the government of Russia as it encouraged the tsar to work with the *dumas*, but ultimately it seriously weakened the position of the tsar.

The tsar's decision to take over command of the war and move to the front was a serious political mistake. It meant that he left the running of the country in the hands of his wife, Alexandra, the tsarina. She refused to take advice from middle-class members of the *duma* and they became increasingly frustrated.

During the war, the Russian people grew to hate anything German. They changed the name of their capital city from the German St Petersburg to the Russian Petrograd. Alexandra was German and it was rumoured that she was a German spy trying to sabotage the Russian war effort.

Rasputin was the only person Alexandra was prepared to listen to. Indeed, he seemed to be in charge of the government. The tsarina frequently dismissed any capable ministers from the *duma* on Rasputin's advice and replaced them with his friends, who were totally incompetent. There were so many changes of ministers that nobody was organising food, fuel and other supplies to the cities properly. The railway system fell into chaos and trainloads of food were left rotting.

As news from the war got worse and the situation in the cities got more desperate, support for the tsar and his wife began to decrease among the middle and upper classes. They blamed the tsar for leaving the country under the control of a German woman influenced by a mad monk.

Source C: Rasputin at a tea party

The death of Rasputin

Rasputin's murder by members of the royal family illustrates the extent of discontent in Russia, especially with Rasputin's influence over Alexandra. Indeed, members of the royal family begged Alexandra to dismiss Rasputin. When she refused, some, led by Prince Yusupov, in desperation, decided to assassinate him. One evening in December 1916, Rasputin was invited to Yusupov's mansion for a social evening. During the course of the evening he ate cakes laced with enough cyanide to kill several men. He collapsed but then stood up and ran into the courtyard. There he was shot twice. His hands were bound behind him and his body was thrown into the icy river where he drowned.

You do not need to know the details of his murder for this topic. However, you may wish to carry out your own further research on the mystery surrounding the exact circumstances of his death.

Tasks

1. Study Source B. How serious was the situation in Petrograd at the end of 1916?

2. Explain the economic and social effects of the war on Russia in the years 1914–16.

3. Read about Rasputin's death. Then devise an eye-catching headline in a Russian newspaper announcing Rasputin's death.

4. Look at the circles below. This is known as a Venn diagram. They are used to show how factors can overlap with each other – how one factor can influence another.

Sketch your own Venn diagram and use it to show the overlap between the military, political, economic/social effects. One example has been done for you, showing the leadership of Rasputin and the tsarina.

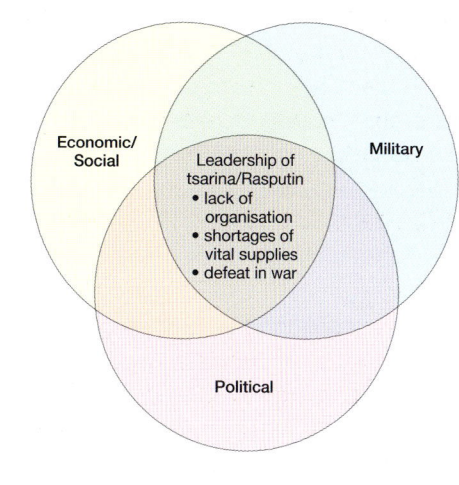

Chapter 2 The impact of the First World War

Examination practice

This section provides guidance on how to answer question 1a from Unit 2, which is worth four marks. This is the source inference question.

Question 1 – source inference
What can you learn from Source A about the situation in Russia at the beginning of 1917? (4 marks)

How to answer
- You are being asked to give the message or messages of the source, to read between the lines of what is written.
- In addition, you must support the inference. In other words, use details from the source to support the messages you say it gives.
- Begin your answer with 'This source suggests…'
- Look for key words in the source that might lead to inferences. You could tackle this by copying the source and highlighting different messages in different colours to help identify messages (as in the example below).
- Avoid repeating the content of the source.
- For maximum marks you will need to make at least two supported references. For example, in Source A two messages could be:

Inference
The source suggests that the war has caused inflation.
Support from the source
High cost of living, prices have gone up.

Source A
There was a total lack of patriotic feeling amongst the majority of the working classes and an increasing number of strikes. This was due to the high cost of living and the increasing shortages of food, clothing and footwear. By the end of 1916 prices were five to ten times greater than in the year 1915.

Inference
Source A suggests that there is growing opposition to the Tsar and the war.
Support from the source
A total absence of patriotic feeling, there is an increase in strikes.

Source A: From a history of Russia, published in 1996

There was a total lack of patriotic feeling amongst the majority of the working classes and an increasing number of strikes. This was due to the high cost of living and the increasing shortages of food, clothing and footwear. By the beginning of 1917 prices were five to ten times greater than in the year 1915.

Source B: From a history of Russia, published in 1996

As the news from the war got worse and the situation in the cities got more desperate, support for the Tsar and his wife began to decrease among the upper and middle classes of society and even among the aristocracy. They were appalled that a man like Rasputin should be allowed such influence and they had little respect for the Tsarina.

Question 2 – source inference
What can you learn from Source B about attitudes to Tsar Nicholas and Tsarina Alexandra by the beginning of 1917? (4 marks)

Now have a go yourself
Try answering question 2 using the steps shown for question 1.

3 The fall of the tsar and the establishment of the Provisional Government

Source A: From a letter written in February 1917 by a 14-year-old boy describing the situation in Petrograd

Terrible things are happening in Petrograd. It has become a real battlefield. Five regiments of the army have joined the revolt. Gunfire never ceases in our part of the city. The officers cannot go into the streets, because the crowd disarms them and even kills them. . . Worst of all, the soldiers have got hold of vodka and are drunk.

Source B: From the diary of Sybil Grey, an English woman living in Petrograd. The entry was dated 23 February 1917

Today I saw a poor woman enter a bread shop and ask for bread. She was told there was none. On leaving the shop, seeing some bread in the window, she broke the glass and took the bread. A general, passing in his motor car, stopped and told her off. A crowd collected round them and smashed his car.

Task

What can you learn from Sources A and B about the situation in Petrograd in February 1917?

By the beginning of January 1917, the position in Russia was becoming chaotic. Defeats in the war, food shortages and lack of social and political reform meant that support for the tsar had been severely eroded. At the end of February, Nicholas **abdicated** and a **Provisional Government** was set up to run Russia until elections could be held. After the elections, a permanent government would be established. The Provisional Government had some successes initially but, by the autumn of 1917, it was challenged by the Bolsheviks and, in October, the Bolsheviks seized power.

This chapter will answer the following questions:

- Why was there a revolution in Russia in February 1917?
- What were the weaknesses and failures of the Provisional Government?
- What was the significance of the Kornilov Revolt?

Examination skills

This chapter gives guidance on question 1b from Unit 2. This question, which is worth six marks, is a describe question. It usually asks you to describe the key features of actions or events in a given period.

Why was there a revolution in Russia in February 1917?

Source A: From a letter written by Grand Duke Michael to the tsar in January 1917. He was describing the problems facing Russia at that time

The unrest continues to grow. Those who defend the idea that Russia cannot exist without a tsar are losing the ground under their feet, since the facts of disorganisation and lawlessness are obvious. A situation like this cannot last long. It is impossible to rule the country without paying attention to the voice of the people and without meeting their needs.

Source B: Table showing prices in Petrograd, 1914 and 1916 (figures are in roubles)

Item	1914	1916
Rent for part of a room	2–3 per month	8–12 per month
Dinner in a tea room	0.15–0.20	1 or 2
Tea in a tea room	0.07	0.35
A pair of boots	5–6	20–30
Shirt	0.75–0.90	2.50–3.00

As you have learnt in Chapter 2, the First World War placed a tremendous strain on the tsarist system and, by early 1917, it seemed as if the country was on the verge of collapse. It had been hoped that the murder of Rasputin in December 1916 would help to bring some stability to the running of the country – it did not. The winter weather was especially severe in December and January, and this meant that food supplies to cities and towns were affected. Prices rose and rationing only led to further discontent. In Petrograd, there were strikes and people began to demand food.

Support for Tsar Nicholas continued to diminish and it seemed as if there were no solutions to the many problems facing Russia. The fact that someone like the Grand Duke Michael (Source A) could mention the idea of a direct challenge to the tsar was an indication of the severity of the situation.

Strikes became an everyday occurrence in Petrograd in early 1917 and this resulted in huge numbers of people on the streets. The situation worsened when the soldiers **garrisoned** in Petrograd **mutinied** and began to take sides with the demonstrators. For Nicholas, this was disastrous. A loyal army had saved him in 1905 (see page 14) – now his final pillar of support started to crumble.

Source C: From a January 1917 *Okhrana* report, describing the mood in Petrograd

The proletariat of the capital is on the verge of despair. Time wasted in queues hoping for food to arrive, the increasing death rate due to inadequate diet, cold and dampness as a result of lack of coal and firewood have created a situation whereby the mass of industrial workers are quite ready to let themselves go to the wildest excesses of a hunger riot ... the masses led by the more advanced and already revolutionary minded elements, assume an openly hostile attitude towards the government and protest with all the means at their disposal against the continuation of the war.

Nicholas' presence at the front meant that he did not always know exactly what was happening in Petrograd. In January 1917, General Krymov, a Russian army commander on the Eastern Front, informed Rodzianko, the president of the *duma*, that many soldiers had lost faith in Nicholas and they would support the *duma* if it took over. Krymov also told Rodzianko that the Tsarina Alexandra had to be removed from Russian politics. Rodzianko tried to act on this but he found that Nicholas would not accept advice from him or the *duma*, which had been recalled in 1915. Events rapidly spiralled out of control in February 1917.

Source D: From a letter by a British army officer in Petrograd, February 1917

…as certain as anything that the Emperor and Empress are riding for a fall. Everyone – officers, merchants, ladies – talks openly of the absolute necessity of doing away with them.

The events in Petrograd, 14–25 February 1917

14 February – The president of the *duma*, Rodzianko, informed Nicholas that he could no longer rely on his closest supporters in Petrograd.

18 February – A strike at the Putilov engineering works began. The workers wanted higher wages as a result of inflation.

23 February – International Women's Day organised by **socialist** groups. Large numbers of women joined about 100,000 strikers and demonstrators on the streets of Petrograd. Many women chanted simple slogans such as 'Down with hunger!' and 'Bread for the workers!'

24 February – About 200,000 workers on strike.

25 February – Strikes all over the city with about 300,000 demonstrators on the streets. No newspapers were printed and there was no public transport. The police began to show sympathy for the demonstrators.

Source E: International Women's Day demonstration, Petrograd, 1917. The main banner calls for women to establish an assembly and the one at the front says 'Freedom for the Citizens of Russia'

Source F: A photograph of soldiers and demonstrators in Petrograd, 25 February 1917. The slogan on the banner reads 'Down with the monarchy'

Tasks

1. What can you learn from Sources A, B and D about the situation in Petrograd at the beginning of 1917?

2. Study Source C. List the problems facing

a) the people of Petrograd and
b) the Russian government in January 1917.

3. In what ways does Source C help you to understand why many Russians had come to oppose the war by 1917?

4. What can you learn from Sources E and F about the extent of unrest in Petrograd in 1917?

Chapter 3 The fall of the tsar and the establishment of the Provisional Government

The events in Petrograd, 26–28 February 1917

26 February – Nicholas instructed the army to restore order but some of the Petrograd garrison had deserted. Some shots were fired on the demonstrators. There were no printers to produce the tsar's proclamations.

27 February – Buildings, shops and restaurants were looted. Most of the Petrograd garrison mutinied. Nicholas ordered the *duma* to dissolve. It did so, but twelve members refused and set up a 'Provisional Committee'. Alexander Kerensky, a Social Revolutionary, demanded that Nicholas abdicate.

First meeting of the Petrograd **Soviet** of Soldiers', Sailors' and Workers' Deputies. The Provisional Committee and the Petrograd Soviet were now running the country.

28 February – The Soviet issued the newspaper *Izvestiya* (The News) and declared its intention to remove the old system of government.

Source G: Telegrams from Rodzianko, president of the *duma*, to Tsar Nicholas on 26 and 27 February 1917

Source H: From the diary of a *duma* deputy, 28 February 1917

Petrograd is without bread, transportation has broken down because of the unusually heavy snow and frosts and principally the war. Ministers have stopped coming to the duma…

The events in Petrograd, March 1917

1 March – The Petrograd Soviet issued Soviet Order Number One, which transferred all authority from army officers to the elected representatives of the soldiers.

2 March – Nicholas decided to return to Petrograd and was met at Pskov, where his leading generals told him that his presence in the capital would do no good. They advised him to abdicate. Nicholas abdicated and refused to nominate his son Alexei as his successor because of his haemophilia. Nicholas' brother, the Grand Duke Michael, was then proposed as the new tsar, but he declined.

3 March – The Provisional Committee renamed itself the Provisional Government and became responsible for running the country.

Telegram of 26 February 1917

The situation is serious. The capital is in a state of anarchy. The government is paralysed; the transportation system has broken down; the supply systems for food and fuel are completely disorganized. General discontent is on the increase. There is disorderly shooting in the streets; some of the troops are firing at each other. It is necessary that some person enjoying the confidence of the country be entrusted immediately with the formation of a new government. There can be no delay. Any hesitation is fatal.

Telegram of 27 February 1917

The situation is growing worse. Measures must be taken, immediately, for tomorrow will already be too late. The final hour has struck, when the fate of the country and the dynasty is being decided. The government is powerless to stop the disorders. The troops of the garrison cannot be relied upon. The reserve battalions of the Guard regiments are in the grips of rebellion, their officers are being killed. Having joined the mobs and the revolt of the people, they are marching on the offices of the Ministry of the Interior and the Imperial Duma. Your Majesty, do not delay. Should the agitation reach the army, Germany will triumph and the destruction of Russia along with the dynasty is inevitable.

The abdication of Tsar Nicholas II

The Romanov dynasty was now at a close and had reached the point where it ended itself. The abdication of Nicholas and the emergence of the Provisional Government out of the *duma* is called the February Revolution. The abdication took place in a railway carriage 320 kilometres from Petrograd (see Source I). The Revolution was over. It had been unplanned and the end of the Romanov dynasty came most unexpectedly.

Source I: The abdication of Nicholas II, March 1917. Nicholas is seated

Source J: From *The History of the Russian Revolution 1930* by L. Trotsky

It would be no exaggeration to say that Petrograd achieved the February Revolution. The rest of the country adhered to it. There was no struggle anywhere except in Petrograd. Nowhere in the country were there any groups of the population, any parties, institutions or military units ready to put up a fight for the old regime. Neither at the front nor at the rear was there a brigade or regiment prepared to do battle for Nicholas II. …Thus ended a reign which had been a continuous chain of ill luck, failure, misfortune, and evil-doing, from the shooting of strikers and revolting peasants, the Russo-Japanese war, the frightful putting-down of the revolution of 1905, the innumerable executions and ending with the insane and contemptible participation of Russia in the insane and contemptible world war…

Tasks

5. Study Source G, Rodzianko's two telegrams to Tsar Nicholas. Can you suggest reasons why Nicholas failed to respond to the growing problems in Petrograd?

6. What can you learn about the abdication of Nicholas II from Source I?

7. Some historians have said that 27 February was the most important day in the Revolution. Why do you think this is the case? Explain your reasons.

8. Re-read pages 25–29. What were the causes of the February Revolution? Make a copy of the following table and place the causes of the Revolution under the column headings and number them in what you think is their order of importance.

Impact of the war	Social problems	Mistakes of tsar	Economic problems	Political problems

9. Re-read Chapters 1, 2 and pages 25–29. What were the causes of the February Revolution? Make a list of the causes of the Russian Revolution under the column headings below.

Long-term causes	Short-term causes

Chapter 3 The fall of the tsar and the establishment of the Provisional Government

What were the weaknesses and failures of the Provisional Government?

The end of tsarism was unplanned and took people by surprise. The Provisional Government was set up on 3 March 1917 and it promised to bring reforms to Russia. There would also be elections for a new **Constituent Assembly** (parliament) as soon as possible. The Provisional Government consisted of a cabinet of minsters (see Source A). The prime minister was Prince Lvov, a wealthy aristocratic landowner, and other leading figures included:

- Milyukov – Foreign Minister and leader of the Cadets
- Guchkov – War Minister and leader of the Octobrists
- Kerensky – Minister of Justice and Social Revolutionary.

The remaining ministers were chosen from the Octobrist and Cadet parties. Thus, the new government was composed of middle-class politicians who wanted to draw up a constitution and establish a democratic government. Initially, it was supported by the Bolsheviks, who believed that the working classes could become better organised under such a government. Then, in the future, the workers would be able to seize power from the middle classes.

The Provisional Government's problems

The Provisional Government faced a number of problems as soon as it was formed:
- it was not a truly elected body and did not represent the people of Russia
- there were defeats in the war
- soldiers were deserting
- peasants were looting the property of the landlords
- soldiers and workers were setting up soviets in towns and cities
- people wanted an end to food shortages
- some of the national minorities, such as the Poles and Finns, were hoping that there might even be a chance of independence in the near future.

Perhaps the most serious issue facing the Provisional Government was the formation of the Petrograd Soviet of Workers' and Soldiers' Deputies. By early March, the Soviet had about 3000 elected members and contained many revolutionaries, especially Socialist Revolutionaries and Mensheviks (see page 16).

The Petrograd Soviet issued Soviet Order Number One (see Source B) and it was this which took away much of the authority of the new government. The existence of the Provisional Government and the Petrograd Soviet meant that there were two bodies running Russia; this became known as the Dual Authority. Both bodies met in the same building, the Tauride Palace. Initially they worked together, but as the months wore on, a gulf between the two began to grow. The Soviet came under the influence of the Bolsheviks, who attacked the Provisional government for continuing the war.

Source A: Collage of photographs of the ministers of the Provisional Government, March 1917

A photograph of the Petrograd Soviet meeting in early 1917

Source B: Soviet Order Number One, 14 March 1917

The Soviet of Workers' and Soldiers' Deputies has resolved:

In all its political actions, troop units are subordinate to the Soviet.

All types of arms must be kept under the control of the company and battalion committees and in no case turned over to officers, even at their demand.

The orders of the State Duma shall be executed only in such cases as do not conflict with the orders of the Soviet of Workers' and Soldiers' Deputies.

In spite of Soviet Order Number One, the Provisional Government decided to continue the war. Russia could only do so if its allies loaned more money and Britain and France were prepared to do this. There were even some Bolsheviks – Stalin and Kamenev – who felt that the war should not be stopped. However, the decision to continue the war was fatal for the Provisional Government because further defeats served only to create unpopularity. A major defeat in June 1917 resulted in more than 60,000 deaths and this led to yet more desertions. When soldiers returned home, they took part in seizing land from the nobility – thus adding to the chaos across Russia.

To add to the misery of the Provisional Government, Germany sent exiled revolutionaries back to Russia in the hope that they would stir up rebellion. Among these was Lenin, the Bolshevik leader, who arrived in Petrograd in April 1917. Lenin began to call for the overthrow of the Provisional Government.

Tasks

1. Look at all the problems that faced the Provisional Government. Copy the table below, placing the problems in the appropriate column, and number them in what you think is their order of importance.

Political problems	Economic problems	Military problems

2. Explain why Soviet Order Number One was so important in undermining the Provisional Government. (For guidance on answering this type of question, see page 74.)

Chapter 3 The fall of the tsar and the establishment of the Provisional Government

The Provisional Government's reforms

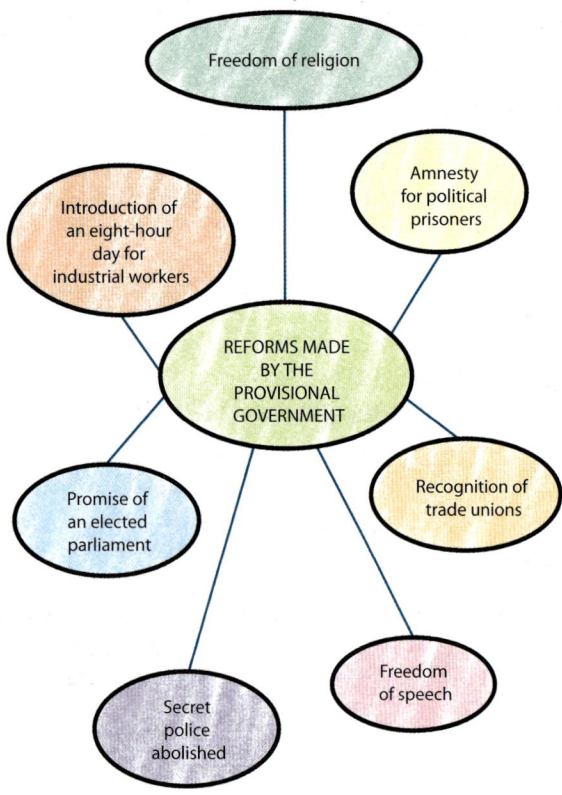

Despite its many problems, the Provisional Government did make some reforms during the early weeks of its ministry. Each reform tried to address problems which had either not been solved after the 1905 Revolution, or had been created by the tsar and his ministers in an effort to keep tight control over the Russian people. The reforms were quite wide-ranging and it was hoped that the workers and the middle classes would be satisfied by them.

However, the decision to continue the war was fatal for the Provisional Government. In May, Guchkov and Milyukov were forced to resign, because they wanted to continue taking part in the war even if German troops were pushed off Russian soil. In the following month, the Russian army suffered heavy casualties in a new offensive against the Germans. Nevertheless, the first **All-Russian Congress of Soviets** meeting in June 1917 gave a vote of confidence in the Provisional Government. (Only 105 out of 822 representatives in the Congress were Bolsheviks.)

The return of Lenin

> **Source A:** From the *Memoirs of Lenin* written by N. Krupskaya (Lenin's wife) published in 1970. Here she is describing Lenin's arrival at the Finland Station
>
> *The Petrograd masses, workers, soldiers and sailors came to meet their leader ... There was a sea of people all around. Red banners, a guard of honour of sailors, searchlights from the fortress of Peter and Paul decorated the road ... armoured cars, a chain of working men and women guarded the road.*

When war broke out in 1914, Lenin was in Austria. He was arrested, but allowed to travel to Zurich in neutral Switzerland. He was utterly opposed to the war, but found that there were many Bolsheviks who supported it. Moreover, there were many socialists in Europe who also supported the war and this seemed to show that Lenin was out of step with current thinking.

After the February Revolution, Lenin was desperate to return to Russia. He was keen that his supporters at home should put forward the message that the Bolsheviks wanted peace and an end to the chaos in Russia. The Germans decided to help Lenin return from exile in Switzerland, in the hope that he would overthrow the new government in Russia. The Germans thought that if Russia pulled out of the war, then more troops could be moved to the Western Front to fight Britain and France.

Lenin was put in a sealed train and sent across Germany and Sweden. He arrived in Petrograd at the Finland Station on 3 April 1917. The price he paid for this method of transport was the accusation that he was a German spy, in the pay of the enemy. Lenin was unconcerned. He had returned and, moreover, the money from the Germans would help finance his revolution.

Task

3. Look at the diagram of the Provisional Government's reforms. Choose the three most important and explain each choice.

Key Topic 1 The collapse of the tsarist regime, 1917

Source B: A 1930s painting of Lenin's arrival at the Finland station in 1917

The April Theses

Lenin made it clear to his followers that he would not support the Provisional Government. He wanted a workers' revolution and his plans were set out the day after his return, in what became known as the April Theses. The Bolsheviks did grow in popularity and, by June 1917, there were more than 40 newspapers spreading Lenin's views and ideas across Russia. The Bolsheviks even had their own '**Red Guard**' – by July, there were about 10,000 armed workers in Petrograd itself.

The April Theses

i) The war with Germany had to end.
ii) Power had to pass from the middle classes to the working classes.
iii) All land had to be given to the peasants.
iv) The police, army and bureaucracy should be abolished.
v) The capitalist system had to be overthrown by the workers – banks, factories and transport should be nationalised.
vi) The Bolsheviks should take control of the soviets in order to achieve their aims. The slogan 'All power to the soviets' became the watchword.

Source C: Membership of the Bolshevik Party, 1917

| February: 24,000 | April: 100,000 | October: 340,000 (60,000 in Petrograd) |

Tasks

4. What can you learn from Sources A and B about the attraction of Lenin in 1917?

5. Construct a table like the one below and explain why each group would support or oppose the April Theses.

APRIL THESES	SUPPORT	OPPOSE
Workers		
Middle classes		
Peasants		
Soldiers		

Chapter 3 The fall of the tsar and the establishment of the Provisional Government

The July Days

> **Source D:** Demonstrators in Petrograd being fired upon by police during the July Days, 1917

Despite the vote of confidence, by July, the Provisional Government was still experiencing problems. The war was not going well and the growing power of the soviets and strength of opposition were key concerns. The Austrian Front was disintegrating and this caused many soldiers to flood back to Russia. For three days, there was chaos in Petrograd when the soldiers and some Bolsheviks tried to overthrow the Provisional Government. Lenin felt that the Bolsheviks had grown sufficiently to challenge the Provisional Government, which had done little to put right the grievances of the people.

The Bolsheviks had their own 'Red Guard' – workers with rifles – and by early July had almost 10,000 in Petrograd, a number which was swelled by army deserters. The riots and disorder were only calmed when Kerensky, the Minister of War, was able to move loyal troops to quash the rebels.

About 400 people were killed and injured during the chaos and Kerensky claimed that the Bolsheviks, who had been involved in the trouble, were all in the pay of Germany. When Lenin fled the country and other leading Bolsheviks were arrested or went into hiding, it appeared that the Bolsheviks' chance to seize power had gone and that the party was in decline.

Consequences of the July Days

- A new government was set up with Kerensky as prime minister. He accused the Bolsheviks of being German spies because he knew that Lenin's return to Russia had been financed by Germany. Moreover, much of the Bolsheviks' revolutionary activity since April had been backed by German money.
- The Bolsheviks were denounced as traitors – their newspaper, *Pravda*, was closed down, Lenin fled the country and Kamenev was arrested.

Source E: A cartoon from *Petrogradskaia Gazeta*, 7 July 1917. The *Gazeta* was a pro-government newspaper. The caption at the top reads 'A high post for the leaders of the rebellion'. The caption below reads 'Lenin wants a high post? ...Well? A position is ready for him!!!'

Source F: Kerensky (left) speaking to troops leaving for the frontline, 1917

Furthermore, Lenin knew that the Russian army could be swayed towards the Bolshevik anti-war policy – the majority of soldiers were really 'peasants in uniform'. The new Bolshevik slogan of 'Peace, Land and Bread' began to attract more and more followers during these critical times. Lenin also used the simple slogan – 'All power to the soviets' and many Bolsheviks came to realise that if they controlled the soviets across Russia then they would come closer to securing power in the country.

However, the Bolsheviks were not finished. Lenin directed them from Finland and they were able to continue to function and maintain their high profile. Lenin altered his views about the peasants and their role in any revolution. He accepted the land seizures and encouraged even more, thus winning support in the countryside. The slogan 'land to the peasants' was continually emphasised by the Bolsheviks.

Tasks

6. *In what ways is Source D helpful in understanding the July Days?*

7. *What can you learn from Source E about the attitude of some of the Petrograd press towards Lenin and the Bolsheviks?*

8. *What does Source F show you about Kerensky in 1917?*

9. *Explain why the July Days were important for the Bolsheviks.* (For guidance on answering this type of question, see page 74.)

Chapter 3 The fall of the tsar and the establishment of the Provisional Government

What was the significance of the Kornilov Revolt?

After the July Days, Alexander Kerensky was appointed the new prime minister. He was determined to continue the war and wait until the elections before any decisions would be made about ending Russia's participation. However, there was growing disquiet among many Russians because little seemed to have changed since the abdication of Tsar Nicholas.

Moreover, the power and influence of the Bolsheviks were growing. By September, they controlled the Moscow Soviet and also dominated the Petrograd Soviet. Party membership was almost 250,000. Furthermore, the involvement of Trotsky had given a tremendous boost to the Bolshevik Party by September.

> **Source A:** From *Worker and Soldier*, a pro-Bolshevik newspaper, August 1917
>
> The Kerensky government is against the people... The people can only be saved by the completion of the revolution, and for this purpose the full power must be in the hands of the Soviets.
> All power to the Soviets
> Immediate truce on all fronts
> Landlord estates to the peasants
> Workers' control over industrial production
> A Constituent Assembly

General Kornilov inspecting Russian troops in July 1917

The limited power and control of the Provisional Government was shown in the Kornilov Revolt. There is some debate about the events surrounding the Revolt but some points are clear.

In September 1917, General Kornilov, the Supreme Commander-in-Chief of the Russian armed forces, threatened to seize power in Petrograd. Kornilov did not agree with the Petrograd Soviet's wish to end the war and he sought to set up a **military dictatorship**. He would ensure that there was no anarchy or socialist-style government in Russia. If Russia was to defeat Germany, then there had to be stability at home. Kornilov said he would help to restore order.

> **Source B:** From a speech by Kornilov in August 1917
>
> It is time to hang the German supporters and spies, with Lenin at their head, and to disperse the Soviet of Workers' and Soldiers' Deputies far and wide. I have no personal ambition, I only wish to save Russia, and will gladly submit to a strong Provisional Government purified of all undesirable elements.

The position worsened at the end of August and early September when German forces began to threaten Petrograd. Furthermore, the number of deserters and refugees flooding into Petrograd heightened the crisis. In one leaflet to the people of Petrograd entitled 'Don't Believe the Whispers!' the Bolsheviks clearly pointed out the threat posed by Kornilov and urged Russians to stand united against him. The Bolsheviks claimed that Kornilov was helping the Germans and that all he wanted was to seize power for himself and 'overthrow the people's power'.

> **Source C:** From General Kornilov's telegram to Kerensky, 27 August 1917
>
> People of Russia! Our great motherland is dying. I, General Kornilov, declare that under pressure of the Bolshevik majority in the Soviets, the Provisional Government is acting in complete accord with the plans of the German General Staff. It is destroying the army and is undermining the very foundations of the country. The heavy sense of the inevitable ruin of our country forces me to call upon all the Russian people in these terrible times to come to the aid of the dying motherland.

Kornilov then decided to march on Petrograd to save the Provisional Government. (There is some evidence to show that Kerensky asked Kornilov to march on Petrograd but then changed his mind.) To win support and clearly explain his aims, Kornilov issued his own manifesto which:

- attacked the Bolsheviks in the Petrograd Soviet
- asked for the war to be continued
- called for the meeting of a Constituent Assembly.

Kornilov was immediately condemned by Kerensky, and Petrograd was placed under martial law. As Kornilov and his forces approached Petrograd, Kerensky allowed the Bolshevik **Red Guards** to arm and was happy to see the Bolsheviks persuade many of Kornilov's troops to desert. Kerensky also set free many Bolsheviks who had been imprisoned after the July Days, so that there would be a considerable force to oppose Kornilov in Petrograd.

Railway workers prevented Kornilov's troops from approaching Petrograd and printers stopped publication of newspapers that supported the *coup d'etat*. The attempted coup failed and Kornilov was arrested.

Consequences of the Kornilov Revolt

Following the revolt, Kerensky's government looked rather weak (see Source A) and the Bolsheviks, who had secured control of the Petrograd where Trotsky was now chairman of the Petrograd Soviet, were in the ascendancy. Many of their followers were armed and those imprisoned in July were free – many of the Bolsheviks began to sense that their time was approaching.

With the arrest of Kornilov, the Army High Command had lost its commander-in-chief and morale sank even lower. Moreover, officers continued to be murdered and desertions reached an even higher level. The army was no longer in a position to set up a military dictatorship.

> **Tasks**
>
> 1. Study Source A. What criticisms was the newspaper making about the Provisional Government?
>
> 2. Study Sources B and C. What were Kornilov's aims?
>
> 3. Suggest reasons why the Bolsheviks entitled their pamphlet 'Don't Believe the Whispers!'
>
> 4. Why did the Kornilov Revolt fail?
>
> 5. Did Kornilov and the Bolsheviks agree on any issues at this time?

Source D: From *The Russian Revolution* by D. Footman, 1962

*After the Kornilov Revolt, Kerensky and his cabinet were still in power. But there had been a striking change in the mood throughout the country. The Bolsheviks could now claim to have been the leaders in the 'victory over the **counter-revolution**' and their power and influence increased rapidly.*

All the problems that the Provisional Government had faced in February had not gone away and by October it retained little authority. Lenin's promises of 'Peace, Bread, Land' were proving more attractive than the seeming inaction of Kerensky. It is ironic that when Kerensky did act – setting the date of the elections for the Constituent Assembly – it pushed Lenin to decide on a takeover.

Source E: From Lenin's letter, from Finland, to the Bolshevik Central Committee, September 1917

The Bolsheviks, having obtained a majority in the Soviets of Workers' and Soldiers' Deputies in Petrograd and Moscow, can and must take state power into their hands. …the Bolsheviks, by immediately proposing a democratic peace, by immediately giving the land to the peasants and by re-establishing the democratic institutions and liberties which have been distorted and shattered by Kerensky, will form a government which nobody will be able to overthrow.

Lenin, in exile in Finland, began to make plans not only for his return to Petrograd but also for the Bolshevik seizure of power. Lenin could now show that the Bolsheviks had helped to save Petrograd and this helped to wipe out memories of the July Days. Lenin and Trotsky acknowledged that the arming of the Red Guard was crucial and the creation of workers' militia during the Revolt would be of great help whenever they decided to seize power. Trotsky and other leading Bolsheviks in Petrograd had become aware during August that public opinion was moving towards them but they also saw that there was a sharp swing after the failure of Kornilov. It was also encouraging that Bolsheviks in other towns and cities reported increased support at this time.

Lenin's famous judgement about the Provisional Government after the failure of the Kornilov Revolt was that it was now 'ripe for the plucking'.

The details and events of the Bolshevik Revolution are to be found in the next chapter.

Tasks

6. Write a brief newspaper article explaining how the Kornilov Revolt helped the Bolsheviks. Begin with a headline of about 6 to 8 words.

7. Working in groups of three, choose which one of the following you consider the most important for the Bolsheviks in 1917 – the April Theses, the July Days or the Kornilov Revolt.

8. Look back over this chapter and complete the following task:

Why was the Provisional Government in a precarious position by 1917? Answer by constructing a diagram as below, with the most important reasons at the top and moving in a clockwise direction.

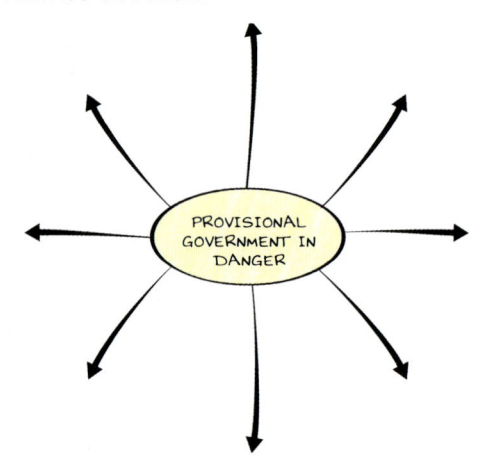

[Diagram: central oval labelled "PROVISIONAL GOVERNMENT IN DANGER" with eight arrows radiating outward]

9. Re-read this chapter, which shows that Tsar Nicholas II and the Provisional Government faced similar problems. Copy the table below and complete the boxes, explaining your answer.

Problems	Worse for Tsar Nicholas II?	Worse for the Provisional Government?

Key Topic 1 The collapse of the tsarist regime, 1917

Examination practice

This section provides guidance on how to answer question 1b from Unit 2, which is worth six marks. There is further guidance on how to answer this type of question on page 48.

Question 1 – describe
Describe the key features of the Kornilov Revolt, September 1917. (6 marks)

How to answer

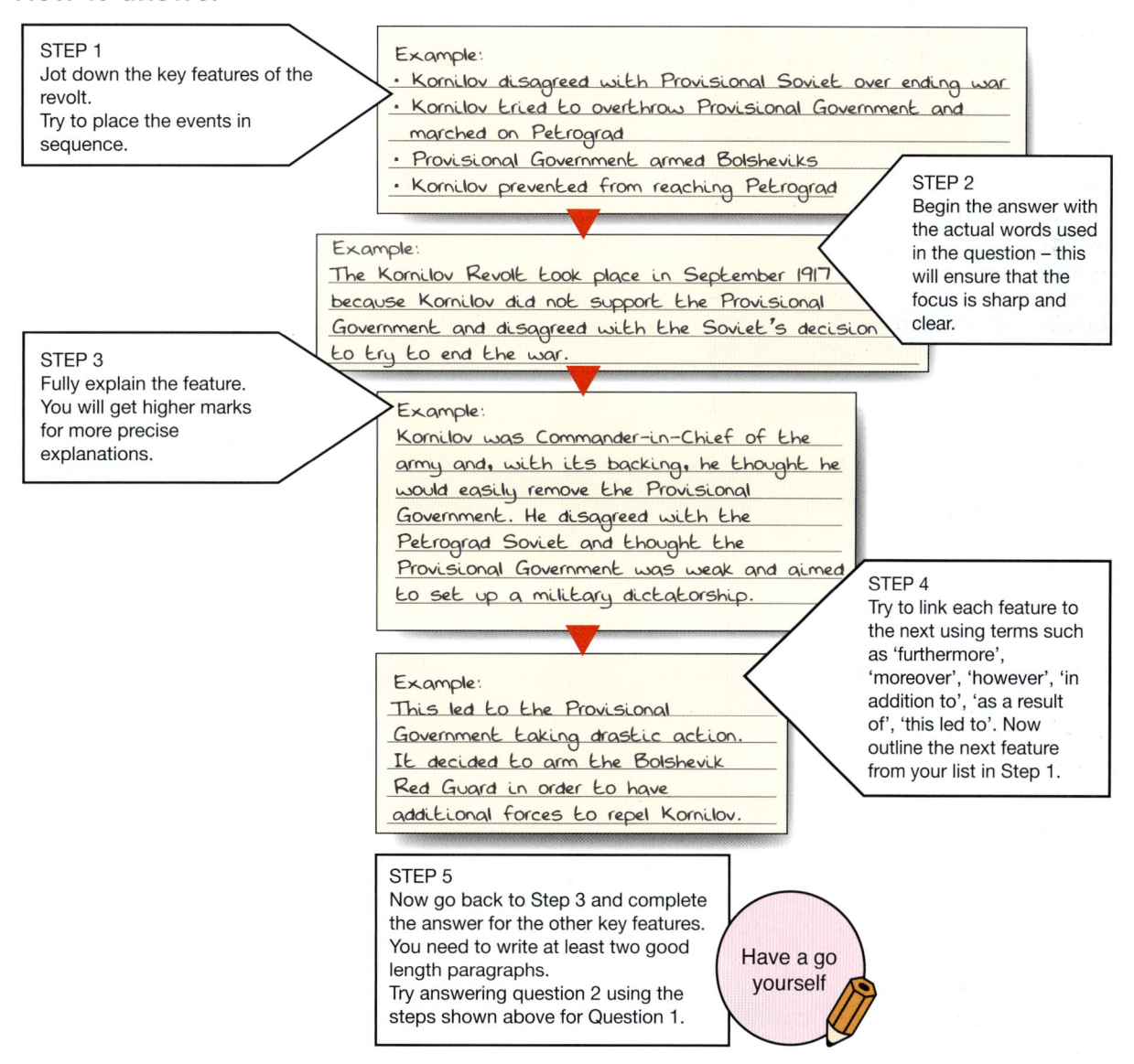

STEP 1
Jot down the key features of the revolt.
Try to place the events in sequence.

Example:
- Kornilov disagreed with Provisional Soviet over ending war
- Kornilov tried to overthrow Provisional Government and marched on Petrograd
- Provisional Government armed Bolsheviks
- Kornilov prevented from reaching Petrograd

STEP 2
Begin the answer with the actual words used in the question – this will ensure that the focus is sharp and clear.

Example:
The Kornilov Revolt took place in September 1917 because Kornilov did not support the Provisional Government and disagreed with the Soviet's decision to try to end the war.

STEP 3
Fully explain the feature. You will get higher marks for more precise explanations.

Example:
Kornilov was Commander-in-Chief of the army and, with its backing, he thought he would easily remove the Provisional Government. He disagreed with the Petrograd Soviet and thought the Provisional Government was weak and aimed to set up a military dictatorship.

STEP 4
Try to link each feature to the next using terms such as 'furthermore', 'moreover', 'however', 'in addition to', 'as a result of', 'this led to'. Now outline the next feature from your list in Step 1.

Example:
This led to the Provisional Government taking drastic action. It decided to arm the Bolshevik Red Guard in order to have additional forces to repel Kornilov.

STEP 5
Now go back to Step 3 and complete the answer for the other key features. You need to write at least two good length paragraphs.
Try answering question 2 using the steps shown above for Question 1.

Have a go yourself

Now have a go yourself
Try answering question 2 using the steps shown above for question 1.

2. Describe the key features of the July Days, 1917. (6 marks)

Key Topic 2: Bolshevik takeover and consolidation, 1917–24

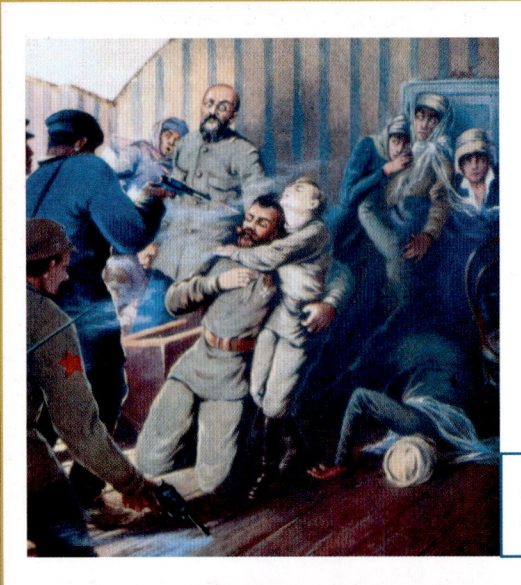

Tasks

1. What does Source A show us about the death of the tsar and his family?
2. What message is the artist trying to put across?

Source A: A painting showing the death of Tsar Nicholas II and his family

This key topic examines the reasons for the **Bolshevik** seizure of power in 1917, especially the roles of Lenin and Trotsky and how the Bolsheviks imposed their rule on Russia in the years 1918–21. In addition, it explains the key changes introduced by Lenin, more especially **War Communism** and the **New Economic Policy**.

Each chapter explains a key issue and examines important lines of enquiry as outlined below:

Chapter 4 The October revolution (pages 41–48)

- How did the Bolshevik Party seize power in 1917?
- What was the role of Trotsky?
- What were the main events of the Bolshevik Revolution?
- What was the role of Lenin?
- Why were the Bolsheviks successful?

Chapter 5 Imposing Bolshevik control, 1917-21 (pages 49–60)

- How did the Bolsheviks secure control?
- Why was the Constituent Assembly dissolved?
- Why was the Treaty of Brest-Litovsk important?
- Why did a civil war break out in 1918?
- Why did the Bolsheviks win the civil war of 1918–21?

Chapter 6 Creating a new society, 1918-24 (pages 61–67)

- Why was there opposition to War Communism?
- Why was there a mutiny at Kronstadt?
- What was the New Economic Policy?
- What were the effects of the New Economic Policy?

4 The October revolution

Source A: P. Sorokin, a Socialist Revolutionary, describing the Bolshevik attack on the Provisional Government on 25 October 1917

I learned that the Bolsheviks had brought up the warship Aurora *and had opened fire on the Winter Palace, demanding the surrender of the members of the Provisional Government still barricaded there . . . There was a regiment of women and young military trainees bravely resisting an overwhelming force of Bolshevik troops . . . Poor women, poor lads, their situation was desperate, for we knew the wild sailors would tear them to pieces.*

Task

What can you learn from Source A about the Bolshevik attack on the Provisional Government in 1917?

The Bolshevik Party seized power in October 1917 with very little opposition. The **Provisional Government** was removed with ease and Lenin established a government based on the ideas of Karl Marx. Although the Bolshevik Party had been quite insignificant before 1905, membership did begin to grow slowly thereafter. The leading Bolsheviks were determined and dedicated and never lost sight of their goal – a revolution that would bring power to the **working classes**. The First World War created the opportunity for their success.

This chapter will answer the following questions:

- How did the Bolshevik Party seize power in 1917?
- What was the role of Trotsky?
- What were the main events of the Bolshevik Revolution?
- What was the role of Lenin?
- Why were the Bolsheviks successful?

Examination skills
This chapter gives you further guidance on question 1b from Unit 2. This question, which is worth six marks, is a describe question. It usually asks you to describe the key features of actions or events in a given period.

How did the Bolshevik Party seize power in 1917?

> **Key features in the development of the Bolshevik Party to 1914**
>
> - Formed in 1903, following the split in the Social Democratic Party (see page 16)
> - Led by Lenin who put forward his own interpretation of Marxism.
> - Played little part in the 1905 Revolution (see page 14)
> - Lenin instructed the Bolsheviks to boycott the elections for the 1906 *duma*.
> - After 1906, Lenin fought desperately to keep the party and spirit of revolution alive. Party funds were built up by a series of robberies – called 'expropriations' – and hundreds took place each year before 1914.
> - Pre-1914, Bolshevik membership never exceeded 10,000.
> - In 1914, the *Okhrana* (secret police) reported that the Bolsheviks were not a strong threat to tsarism.

You have already read in Chapter 3 about the return of Lenin from exile and how he put forward his ideas of a revolution in the April Theses (page 33). The Bolsheviks began to grow in popularity in 1917 and were also able to form their own army – the **Red Guard** (see page 37).

The decision to seize power

The July Days (see page 34) caused problems for the Bolsheviks, because Lenin was exiled again. However, following the Kornilov Revolt (see pages 36–38), Lenin began to contemplate his return to Russia in order to begin his long-awaited revolution. In his words, the Provisional Government was 'ripe for plucking'.

Because of the Kornilov Revolt, the Bolsheviks were able to say that they were the true defenders of Petrograd. Above all, the Red Guard had retained the weapons given to them by Kerensky.

The **All-Russian Congress of Soviets** was due to meet in late October and it was possible that the Bolsheviks would not have a majority of representatives in it. If, however, the Bolsheviks overthrew the Provisional Government before this, they could present their new authority as a *fait accompli,* which the Congress would find difficult to reject.

Furthermore, Lenin was also aware that the Bolsheviks were unlikely to win a majority of seats in the **Constituent Assembly** – but if they were in power before the elections, then the results could be ignored if they were unfavourable.

Lenin was calling for a revolution, but he still remained in Finland, despite the fact that the Provisional Government had released all political prisoners who had been arrested in July. In September, Lenin wrote 'History will not forgive us if we do not assume power.'

He finally returned to Petrograd on 7 October and then went into hiding. On 10 October, Lenin persuaded the Bolshevik Central Committee to agree in principle on an uprising, but two influential leaders – Kamenev and Zinoviev – voiced strong objections. These two published their objections in a newspaper, alerting Kerensky to the Bolshevik threat. Lenin was furious.

On 23 October, Kerensky tried to remove the Bolshevik threat – he closed down the Bolshevik papers (*Pravda* and *Izvestiya*) and attempts were made to round up leading Bolsheviks. The Bolsheviks were forced into action and Lenin ordered the revolution to begin before Kerensky could capture them. Thus, ironically, Kerensky had decided the exact timing of the revolution.

> **Tasks**
>
> **1.** *Explain why Lenin decided to begin the revolution in October. (For guidance on answering this type of question, see page 74.)*
>
> **2.** *Why did Kerensky think it important to close down the Bolshevik newspapers in October?*

What was the role of Trotsky?

Biography Leon Trotsky 1879–1940

1879 Born Lev Davidovich Bronstein
1897 Involved in organising the South Russian Workers' Union
1898 Arrested and spent four years in exile in Siberia
1902 Escaped and fled to London, assuming the name Trotsky
1902 Joined the Social Democratic (SD) Party. Met and worked with leading SD members
1903 Followed Martov and became a **Menshevik**
1905 Returned to St Petersburg and was eventually elected Chairman of the **Soviet**
1905 Arrested and imprisoned
1906 Exiled to Siberia but escaped after two years
1914 Moved to Zürich and then Paris, where he denounced the war and encouraged workers not to fight
1916 Deported to Spain and then went to the USA
1917 Returned to Russia in May
1917 Chairman of Petrograd Soviet in September and member of **Military Revolutionary Committee (MRC)**
1917 **Commissar** for Foreign Affairs
1918 Commissar for War

As you can see from his biographical details, Trotsky was in exile at the time of the February Revolution. On his return to Russia in May 1917, he was concerned that many Mensheviks were supporting the Provisional Government. He was arrested in July as a result of his revolutionary activities and the following month he became an official Bolshevik Party member.

When the Bolsheviks secured control of the Petrograd Soviet, Trotsky was elected as its leader and this became the key to his success. In October, he became the dominant member of the three-man Military Revolutionary Committee (MRC) of the Soviet. This provided a useful screen for his secret preparations. The MRC – in theory – controlled 20,000 Red Guards, 60,000 Baltic sailors and the 150,000 soldiers of the Petrograd garrison.

From his office in the Smolny Institute, a building formerly used as a girls' school, Trotsky made his plans for the seizure of the key buildings of the Provisional Government.

In October, the Bolsheviks began to reduce their massive demonstrations and street skirmishes, because the crowds were not always easy to control. When they started preparing for the revolution, they began to rely more on small, disciplined units of soldiers and workers. The Bolsheviks, under the leadership of Trotsky, prepared for their overthrow of the Provisional Government on 24 October.

Source A: From *Memoirs of a Revolutionary* by Victor Serge. Serge was a Bolshevik, writing in 1945 about Trotsky

I first saw Trotsky at a packed meeting of the Petrograd Soviet. He was all tension and energy. He outshone Lenin through his **oratorical** talent, his organising ability, first with the army and then with the railways, and by his brilliant gift as a student of political theory ...

Source D: From a speech by Trotsky to the Petrograd Soviet, 22 October 1917

The Soviet government will give everything the country has to the poor and to the soldiers at the front ... We will defend the cause of the workers and peasants to the last drop of blood.

Source B: Photograph of Bolsheviks outside the Smolny Institute, Petrograd, October 1917

Source C: From *History of the Russian Revolution*, written by Trotsky in 1932. He was describing his time in the Smolny Institute during October 1917

The Smolny Institute was being transformed into a fortress. In the top floor there were about two dozen machine-guns. All the reports about the movements of troops, the attitude of soldiers and workers, the agitation in the barracks, the happenings in the Winter Palace – all these came to the Smolny.

Tasks

1. What can you learn from Source A about the character of Trotsky? (Remember how to answer this type of question? For further guidance, see page 24.)

2. Do Sources B and C support each other about Bolshevik forces in October 1917?

3. Using the information on page 47 and Sources A–D on this page, explain Trotsky's role in preparing the Bolsheviks in September and October for revolution.

What were the main events of the Bolshevik Revolution?

> **Source A:** From Lenin, on the eve of the Bolshevik Revolution, urging his colleagues to do what in fact they were doing!
>
> The situation is extremely critical. Delaying the uprising now really means death ... We must at any price, tonight arrest the Ministers and we must disarm the military cadets ... We must not wait! We may lose everything! ... The government is tottering. We must deal it the death blow at any cost.

On the night of 24 October, Trotsky's plans were put into action. Key buildings, such as telegraph offices and railway stations, were captured by the Bolsheviks, and road blocks were set up on the city's bridges and surrounding the Winter Palace, where the Provisional Government was in session. There was little resistance and the citizens of Petrograd went about their everyday business.

Kerensky escaped from Petrograd on the morning of 25 October and tried to raise troops from the front, while the rest of the government remained in the Winter Palace. He could secure no further help. The troops guarding the Provisional Government – the Women's Battalion (known as the Amazons) and the military cadets – surrendered. When the cruiser *Aurora* sailed up the River Neva and fired its guns, the Provisional Government gave in and was placed under arrest. Some of its members were able to slip away unnoticed. In all, the actions of the day had ended with the death of six soldiers, eighteen arrests and the collapse of the Provisional Government.

The Bolsheviks take power

Meanwhile, the All-Russian Congress of Soviets was assembling at the Smolny Institute. The Bolsheviks held the most seats – 390 of 650. The SR and Menshevik representatives condemned the Bolshevik takeover, because it was not a Soviet takeover of power. The two sets of representatives left the Congress and the Bolsheviks' position was strengthened because of their huge majority.

The following day, Lenin formed a government called the Council of People's Commissars. This had an all-Bolshevik membership:
- Lenin was the head of the government
- Trotsky was Commissar of Foreign Affairs
- Stalin was Commissar for Nationalities.

> **Source B:** An artist's interpretation of a poster, dated 5 November 1917, written by Lenin, announcing that the Bolsheviks had removed the Provisional Government
>
> **To the Citizens of Russia!**
>
> The Provisional Government has been deposed. Power has passed into the hands of the Petrograd Soviet of Workers' and Soldiers' Deputies – the Military Revolutionary Committee, which leads the Petrograd proletariat and the garrison. The causes for which the people have fought – peace, the abolition of land ownership, workers' control over production and the establishment of Soviet power have been secured.
>
> **Long live the revolution of the workers, soldiers and peasants!**

Tasks

1. Study Source A. If Lenin was 'urging his colleagues to do what in fact they were doing!', what can you learn about Lenin at this time?
2. Study Source B. Why was Lenin careful to address the poster to 'workers, soldiers and peasants'?

What was the role of Lenin?

Biography Vladimir Illich Ulyanov (assumed name Lenin) 1870-1924

Key events to 1917:
- 1870 Born Vladimir Illich Ulyanov
- 1887 Elder brother, Alexander, hanged as a conspirator in the attempted assassination of Tsar Alexander III
- 1897 Exiled to Siberia – adopted the name Lenin
- 1898 Married Nadezhda Krupskaya
- 1902 Wrote 'What is to be done?' in which he put forward the central role of dedicated party members in any revolution
- 1903 Led the Bolsheviks in the Social Democrat Party split
- 1906 Exiled for much of the next eleven years
- 1912 Secured control of the Central Committee (the body responsible for making policies)
- 1917 Returned to Russia
- 1917 Returned to Russia and led the Bolshevik Revolution

Lenin had tremendous energy and vitality and his commitment to revolution spurred on the Bolsheviks. His decision to oppose the war was the key reason why Bolshevik support rose throughout 1917. He created the Red Guard and brought German money, which helped to equip them. Lenin persuaded the majority of the Central Committee to seize power in October. Trotsky organised the takeover, but without Lenin the Bolsheviks would not have even tried to remove the Provisional Government. Within a week of the revolution in Petrograd, the Bolsheviks took control of Moscow and then began the work of securing control of the whole of Russia.

Source A: A cartoon showing Lenin sweeping away his opponents. The caption reads 'Lenin cleans the earth of evil spirits'

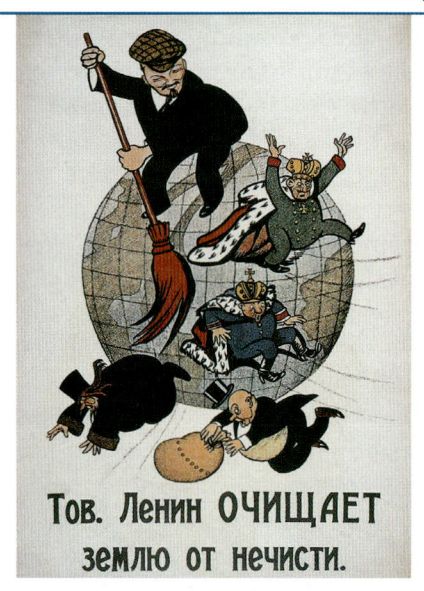

The role of Lenin was crucial. Lenin persuaded the Bolsheviks to oppose the war, unlike the Mensheviks and Socialist Revolutionaries. These two parties were still following Marx's ideas that the workers' revolution was many years away – Lenin had already changed his views in the April Theses (see page 33). He gave the Bolsheviks simple slogans such as 'Peace, Land and Bread' and 'All power to the Soviets'. These were easily understood by the ordinary people.

Tasks

1. Re-read the section above on Lenin and also pages 32–33 about his return in April 1917 and the following months. Construct a concept map of his contribution to the Bolshevik Revolution.

2. Study Source A. Which groups in society are being swept away by Lenin?

Why were the Bolsheviks successful?

The weaknesses of the Provisional Government

The Provisional Government was weak and really only a temporary body. It had not been elected by the people of Russia. Moreover, it had had to share power in Petrograd with the Soviet from the beginning and could not overturn Soviet Order Number One (see page 31).

Kerensky was never able to remove the Bolsheviks completely and during the Kornilov Revolt he had actually armed them. As 1917 unfolded, the Provisional Government was unable to win over the support of ordinary people in Petrograd – the Bolsheviks and other parties were able to publish so much propaganda that when the crisis came in October, Kerensky received little or no help.

> **Source A:** From *Reaction and Revolution* by M. Lynch, 1992
>
> The failure of the Provisional Government to rally effective military support in its hour of need was symptomatic of its much deeper failure over the previous eight months… Kerensky's government came nowhere near to solving Russia's problems or satisfying her needs. Hence its support evaporated…militarily disastrous, the Provisional Government was not considered to be worth struggling to save.

Bolshevik control of the armed forces

Trotsky claimed that the Bolsheviks were successful because the soldiers of the Petrograd garrison did not side with the Provisional Government. Furthermore, the creation of the Military Revolutionary Committee enabled the Bolsheviks to control some of the armed forces at a critical time.

> **Source B:** From an article by Joseph Stalin in *Pravda*, 6 November 1918
>
> All the work of practical organisation of the revolution was conducted under the immediate leadership of the Chairman of the Petrograd Soviet, Trotsky. It is possible to declare with certainty that the swift passing of the garrison to the side of the Soviet and the bold execution of the Military Revolutionary Committee, the Party owes principally and above all to Comrade Trotsky.

Lack of alternatives

The many political parties did not offer clear leadership during 1917. They all became discredited because they supported the continuation of the war. This led to discontent within the army and began to make it increasingly unreliable. The elections to the Constituent Assembly were delayed and the peasants' demand for land was not addressed. Consequently, anarchy and the seizing of land in the countryside increased as 1917 wore on, and left-wing agitators infiltrated the army and destroyed the morale of the soldiers.

> **Tasks**
>
> **1.** What can you learn from Source A about Kerensky and the Provisional Government in late 1917. (Remember how to answer this type of question? For further guidance, see page 24.)
>
> **2.** Working in small groups, choose one of the following options and prepare a case for class discussion. Ensure that you use the sources and information from this chapter and also Chapter Three.
>
> - Lenin was the key to Bolshevik success.
> - Trotsky was the key to Bolshevik success.
> - The mistakes of the Provisional Government were the key to Bolshevik success.

Chapter 4 The October revolution

Examination practice

This section provides guidance on how to answer question 1b from Unit 2, which is worth six marks. There is further guidance on how to answer this type of question on page 39.

Question 1 – describe

Describe the key features of the role of Trotsky in the Bolshevik Revolution. (6 marks)

How to answer

- Underline key points in the question.
- Plan your answer. Think of the relevant points – the main question word is 'describe', and the topic is Trotsky's role. You will need to describe three key features.
- Fully develop each factor/feature you mention. Features could include:
  - Trotsky's character
  - Chairman of the Petrograd Soviet
  - Member of the Military Revolutionary Committee
  - Around when Lenin was in exile

The more precise your knowledge, the higher your marks.

- Make links between one factor/feature and the next. Use link words or phrases, such as 'furthermore', 'moreover', 'however', 'in addition', 'as a result of', and 'this led to'.
- Aim for two good length paragraphs, as the question is worth six marks.

The diagram below shows the steps you should take to write a good answer. Use the steps and the examples to complete the answer to the question. Write your answer one paragraph at a time and link the paragraphs where possible.

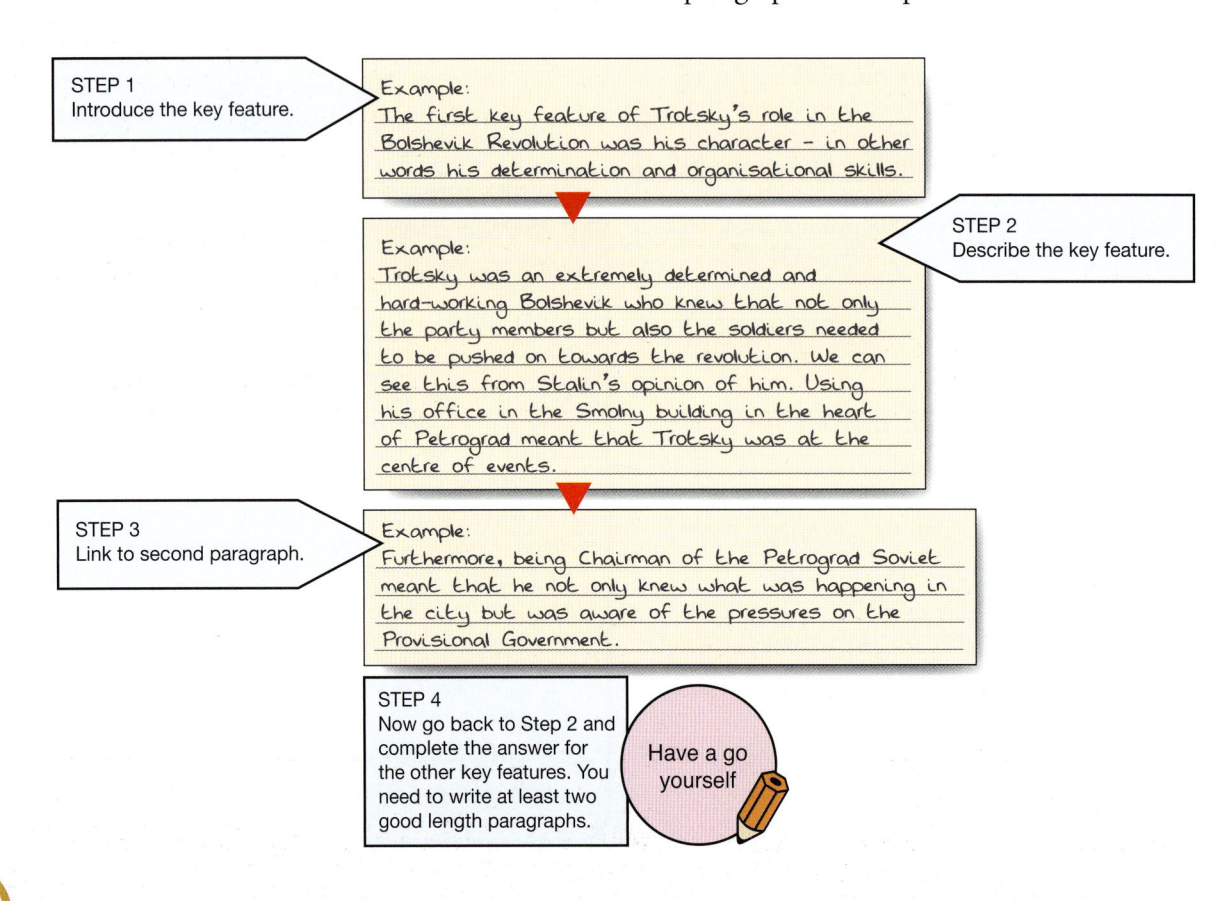

STEP 1 Introduce the key feature.

Example:
The first key feature of Trotsky's role in the Bolshevik Revolution was his character – in other words his determination and organisational skills.

STEP 2 Describe the key feature.

Example:
Trotsky was an extremely determined and hard-working Bolshevik who knew that not only the party members but also the soldiers needed to be pushed on towards the revolution. We can see this from Stalin's opinion of him. Using his office in the Smolny building in the heart of Petrograd meant that Trotsky was at the centre of events.

STEP 3 Link to second paragraph.

Example:
Furthermore, being Chairman of the Petrograd Soviet meant that he not only knew what was happening in the city but was aware of the pressures on the Provisional Government.

STEP 4 Now go back to Step 2 and complete the answer for the other key features. You need to write at least two good length paragraphs.

Have a go yourself

5 Imposing Bolshevik control, 1917–21

Source A: A Bolshevik poster issued soon after the October 1917 Revolution

> **Task**
>
> What message is Source A trying to get across about the Bolshevik Revolution?

The Bolsheviks had seized power with hardly any bloodshed. The Provisional Government literally melted away and Lenin was left to set up a government. However, the Bolsheviks did not have widespread support across Russia and Lenin was keen to impose his control on the country as soon as was feasible. He faced the same problems as the Provisional Government had, and he knew the most pressing issue was Russia's involvement in the war. As Lenin attempted to solve these problems, Russia experienced **civil war**, famine and anarchy in the years to 1921.

This chapter will answer the following questions:

- How did the Bolsheviks secure control?
- Why was the Constituent Assembly dissolved?
- Why was the Treaty of Brest-Litovsk important?
- Why did a civil war break out in 1918?

Examination skills

This chapter gives guidance on question 1c from Unit 2. This question, which is worth eight marks, is a consequence question.

How did the Bolsheviks secure control?

The government that Lenin set up in November 1917 was called Sovnarkom, short for Council of People's Commissars. During the weeks after the Bolshevik takeover, soviets throughout Russia joined in the revolution and took control of most towns and cities. By the end of 1917, nearly all Russia was in soviet hands. This did not mean that Lenin and the Bolsheviks had total control of Russia. Not all the soviets were run by Bolsheviks and, in the countryside, most peasants supported the Socialist Revolutionaries.

Even more awkward from Lenin's point of view, the Provisional Government had arranged for elections to be held in November for a new kind of parliament, called the Constituent Assembly. It seemed that the Socialist Revolutionaries would win more votes than the Bolsheviks. If that happened, the Bolsheviks would have to hand over control of Sovnarkom to their rivals.

On top of these problems, Lenin had to keep promises he had openly made in his April Theses (see page 33) – such as giving land to the peasants.

The first decrees of *Sovnarkom*

Sovnarkom, with Lenin as chairman, issued a series of decrees in November and December 1917.

November decrees

DECREE	DESCRIPTION
Decree on land	540 million acres of land taken from the tsar, the nobles, the Church and other landlords. Peasants to set up committees to divide the land fairly
Decree on unemployment insurance	Employment insurance to be introduced for all workers against injury, illness and unemployment
Decree on peace	*Sovnarkom* intended to make peace immediately with Russia's opponents in the war
Decree on work	An eight-hour day and a 40-hour week for all industrial workers to be introduced. There were restrictions on overtime and there was to be holiday entitlement for workers
Decree on titles	All titles and class distinctions were abolished. Women were declared equal to men
Decree on the press	All non-Bolshevik newspapers were banned

December decrees

DECREE	DESCRIPTION
Decree on workers' control	All factories to be placed under the control of elected committees of workers
Decree to set up the political police	The 'All Russian Extraordinary Commission to fight Counter-Revolution and Espionage' was formed, known as the *Cheka*
Decree on political parties	Russia's main liberal party, the Constitutional Democratic Party, was banned
Decree on banking	All banks in Russia came under *Sovnarkom*'s control
Decree on marriage	Couples could have non-religious weddings and divorce was made easier

Source A: From *The Communist Party of the Soviet Union*, published in 1963. The author, Leonard Schapiro, was describing some of the first actions of the Bolshevik government

Bolshevik practice within a few days of the removal of the Provisional Government was at variance with Lenin's repeated promises. He had said that when they were in power the Bolsheviks would guarantee to each political party which could gather enough supporters the facilities for publishing a newspaper. Some Socialist and Liberal papers, as well as Conservative papers, were closed down in the first few days.

Source B: From the Decree on Education, issued by *Sovnarkom* in 1917

Every genuinely democratic power must, in the sphere of education, make the removal of illiteracy and ignorance its first aim. It must acquire in the shortest time universal literacy by organising a network of schools and it must introduce universal, compulsory and free tuition for all.

Tasks

1. *Describe the key features of the problems Lenin faced when the Bolsheviks first took over in 1917. (Remember how to answer this type of question? For further guidance, see page 39.)*

2. *How useful are Sources A and B for a historian in understanding how the Bolsheviks controlled Russia after 1917?*

3. *Look at the November and December decrees. Copy the table below and fill it in to explain why each section in Russian society would support or oppose the decrees.*

Decree	Worker	Peasant	Middle classes	Nobility

4. *Working in groups, look at the decrees passed by the Bolsheviks in November and December 1917 and discuss the following questions:*

- *Did Lenin follow the April Theses?*
- *In what ways might some people say that Lenin ruled like the tsar?*
- *Was Lenin following the ideas of Marx?*

Chapter 5 Imposing Bolshevik control, 1917–21

Why was the Constituent Assembly dissolved?

Elections were held for Russia's new parliament, the Constituent Assembly, in November 1917. They were the first free elections in Russian history.

The Socialist Revolutionaries (SRs) gained more seats in the Assembly than all the other parties put together (see pie chart below).

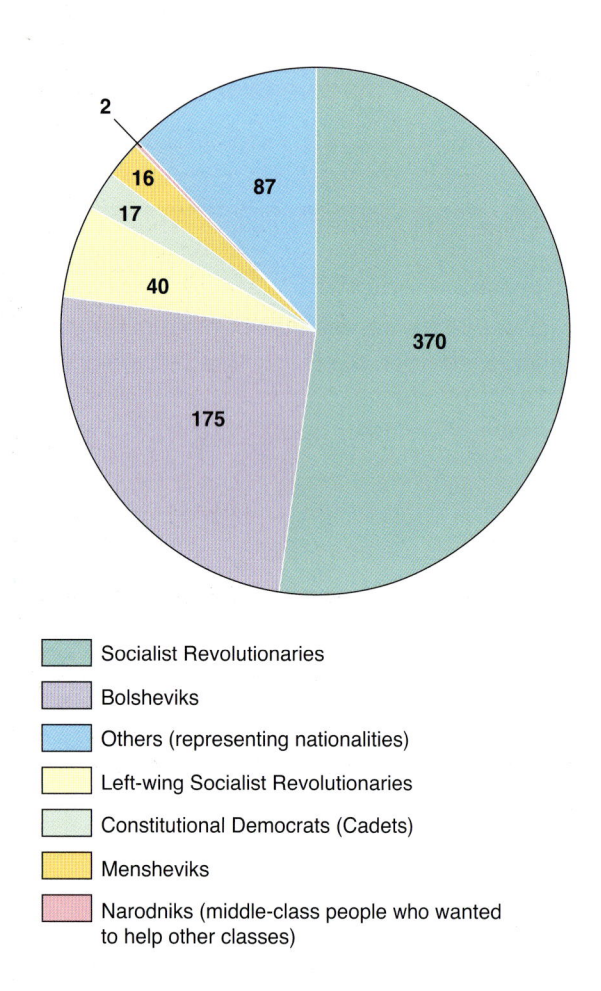

- Socialist Revolutionaries: 370
- Bolsheviks: 175
- Others (representing nationalities): 87
- Left-wing Socialist Revolutionaries: 40
- Constitutional Democrats (Cadets): 17
- Mensheviks: 16
- Narodniks (middle-class people who wanted to help other classes): 2

Number of seats of different parties in the Constituent Assembly, 1917. Total number of seats was 707.

Lenin was concerned that the Bolsheviks had gained only a quarter of the votes and these were primarily from the working classes of the cities. He was also concerned that some of the nationalities, such as Finns and Estonians, were trying to break away and he wanted to avoid the disintegration of Russia.

Lenin wrote an article for *Pravda*, in which he stated that, because there were soviets in Russia, there was no need for the Constituent Assembly.

Nevertheless, the Constituent Assembly met on 18 January 1918. It would have the job of drawing up a new constitution for Russia. The Bolsheviks and the left-wing SRs proposed that the power of the Assembly be limited. When this was defeated, Lenin made his decision to dissolve it.

Less than 24 hours after the Assembly had met, Lenin gave the order to dissolve it. Bolshevik Red Guards killed and wounded more than 100 people who demonstrated in support of the Assembly outside the Tauride Palace. Two leaders of the Cadets were killed in a hospital. The Red Guards then prevented the elected Deputies from entering the Assembly and closed it down permanently. Lenin had removed a threat to the Bolsheviks and *Sovnarkom* at a stroke.

> **Source A:** From a newspaper article written in 1948 by Victor Chernov, leader of the Socialist Revolutionary Party
>
> *When we, the newly elected members of the Constituent Assembly, met on 18 January 1918, we found that the corridors were full of armed guards. Every sentence of my speech was met with outcries, some ironical, others accompanied by the waving of guns. Lenin lounged in his chair with the air of a man who was bored to death.*

> **Source B:** From the memoirs of Edgar Sissons, written in 1931. Sissons was the US Special Representative in Russia in 1918
>
> The Constituent Assembly met in a ring of steel. Armed guards were all about us ... a line of guards stood or walked in the connecting corridor, and at every door was a pair of sailors or soldiers. Even the ushers were armed men.

> **Source C:** From an interview with C. Lindhagen, a Swedish eyewitness at the opening of the Constituent Assembly
>
> In one of the corridors a group of armed soldiers could be glimpsed. I was informed that several of the Deputies (members) as well as the commissars were armed. I asked one of the commissars whether this was true. 'Of course' and he showed me the butt of a revolver in his pocket.

Photograph of the meeting of the Constituent Assembly in the Tauride Palace, January 1918

Tasks

1. What do the election results suggest about the political situation in Russia at the beginning of 1918?

2. How could Lenin justify dissolving the Constituent Assembly? Write a speech in which Lenin explains to the Bolshevik Party why he must dissolve the Constituent Assembly.

3. By January 1918, why were some Russians beginning to compare Lenin, unfavourably, with the tsar? Explain your answer carefully.

4. What similarities and differences are there between Sources A, B and C in their views about the dissolution of the Consituent Assembly? To help you with this answer:

- Make a copy of the following grid.
- Plan your answer using the grid.

	A-B	B-C	A-C
Similarities			
Differences			

5. *Explain why the Constituent Assembly was dissolved by Lenin.* (For guidance on answering this type of question, see page 74.)

Chapter 5 Imposing Bolshevik control, 1917–21

Why was the Treaty of Brest-Litovsk important?

Source A: German troops with the heaped-up bodies of dead Russian soldiers, early 1918

Lenin had opposed the war against Germany from the very beginning, and much of the support the Bolsheviks had gained came from their opposition to the conflict. He was aware that if the Bolsheviks were to hold on to the power they had won in October 1917, then there would have to be an immediate peace settlement. His greatest concern was that any prolongation of the war would mean that the army would not continue to support him.

Source B: Decree on Peace, issued by *Sovnarkom* in November 1917

The workers' and peasants' government proposes to all the warring peoples and their governments that they enter immediately into talks for a just peace. This sort of peace would be an immediate one without seizure of foreign territory and without financial penalties.

Peace talks with Germany began on 3 December 1917 and Lenin sent Trotsky (Commissar for Foreign Affairs) as Russia's representative. Talks were held at Brest-Litovsk, near the German border. Trotsky and his negotiating team tried to prolong the talks as long as possible, because they believed that workers in central Europe were on the brink of revolution. When this revolution came, the war would end and then Germany and Russia would make a fair peace.

As the German army advanced into Russia in February 1918, Lenin's hand was forced and he decided to make peace. The terms of the treaty were the harshest possible and Lenin was heavily criticised by many Bolsheviks. For Lenin and Trotsky, Russia's suffering was a small price to pay for the coming **world socialist revolution**.

Source C: Map showing the territory lost by Russia at the Treaty of Brest-Litovsk. Key population centres, coal mining and iron production areas were in the west

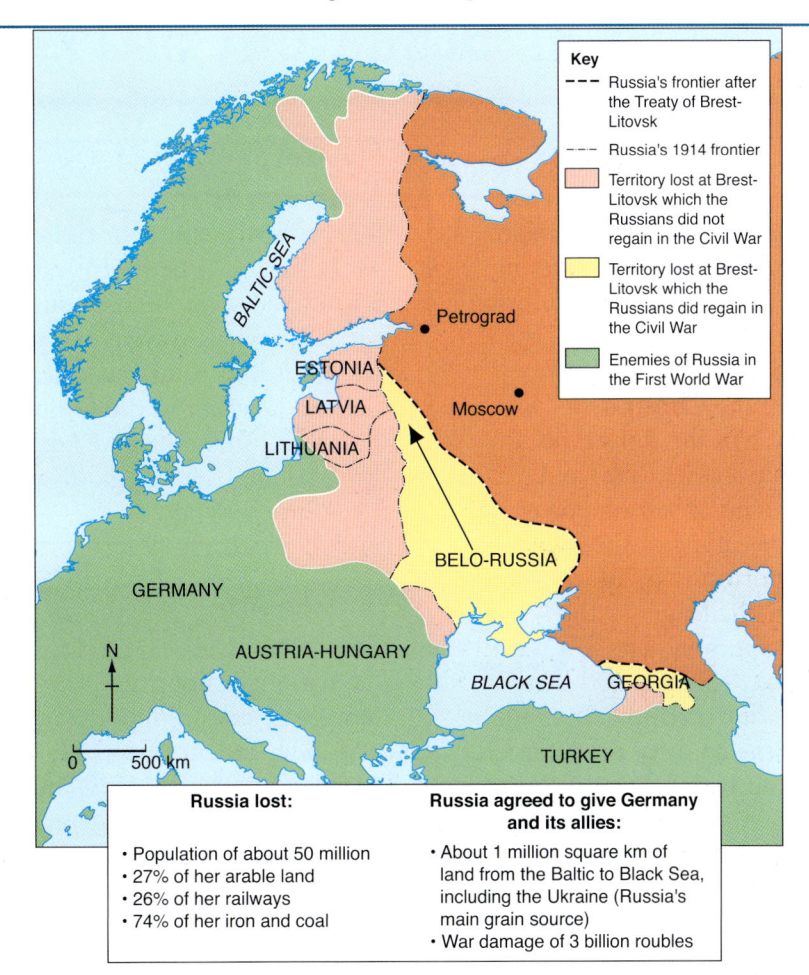

Key
- --- Russia's frontier after the Treaty of Brest-Litovsk
- --- Russia's 1914 frontier
- Territory lost at Brest-Litovsk which the Russians did not regain in the Civil War
- Territory lost at Brest-Litovsk which the Russians did regain in the Civil War
- Enemies of Russia in the First World War

Russia lost:
- Population of about 50 million
- 27% of her arable land
- 26% of her railways
- 74% of her iron and coal

Russia agreed to give Germany and its allies:
- About 1 million square km of land from the Baltic to Black Sea, including the Ukraine (Russia's main grain source)
- War damage of 3 billion roubles

Source D: Lenin speaking in March 1918 about the Treaty of Brest-Litovsk

Our impulse tells us to refuse to sign this robber peace ... Russia can offer no physical resistance because she is materially exhausted by three years of war ... The Russian Revolution must sign the peace to obtain a breathing space to recuperate for the struggle.

Lenin won the debate in the Bolshevik Party about the treaty, but only by the narrowest of margins. His gamble paid off, because with the arrival of US troops and the failure of the German **Spring Offensive**, war in Europe was over in the autumn of 1918 and the Treaty of Brest-Litovsk became meaningless. The defeat of Germany now meant that the treaty had no legality.

However, just as the major danger of Germany was removed, Lenin had to face serious internal threats and, by the spring of 1918, Russia was convulsed by civil war.

Tasks

1. Study Sources A and D and the information on these pages. Explain why Lenin was keen to make a peace settlement with Germany.

2. Study Sources B and C and use your own knowledge about Russia's involvement in the war to list the reasons why Lenin faced opposition to signing the Treaty of Brest-Litovsk.

3. Describe the main terms of the Treaty of Brest-Litovsk. (Remember how to answer this type of question? For further guidance, see page 39.)

Why did a civil war break out in 1918?

The Russian Civil War lasted for almost three years and involved many groups. Furthermore, it was complicated by the involvement of many foreign countries, all of whom had been Russia's allies in the First World War. The civil war seemed to bring together all the problems of the tsarist years, the First World War and the revolutions of 1917.

The decision to dissolve the Constituent Assembly in 1918 did not win the Bolsheviks any friends. The Social Revolutionaries (SRs) and Cadets accused the Bolsheviks of seizing power by force and demanded the re-calling of the Assembly. They were seeking an opportunity to attack the Bolsheviks. In 1918, open challenges to the Bolsheviks became more common. The SRs tried to seize control of the Moscow Soviet and there were even several assassination attempts on Lenin. Sporadic uprisings across the country encouraged anti-Bolsheviks to come out openly against Lenin's regime.

The desperate economic state of many parts of Russia meant that there was still hunger within the country and this led to growing opposition to the Bolsheviks. The starvation worsened after the Brest-Litovsk treaty when the Ukraine was lost, as the Ukraine was the main provider of grain for Russia.

The different groups that opposed the Bolsheviks are explained in the following boxes:

The Czech Legion

There is no specific date that marks the start of the civil war but, by May 1918, events escalated when the Czech Legion revolted. Around 50,000 Czechs, who were prisoners of war in Russia, seized control of the Trans-Siberian railway and began to head for Moscow. They attacked the Red Army and were able to drive Bolshevik troops out of Siberia.

The Whites

The collective name for those who opposed the Bolsheviks (the Reds) was the Whites. The Whites had some military support from ex-tsarist officers and were in a position to fight the Bolsheviks – for example, there was General Denikin in the Caucasus, General Yudenich in Estonia and Admiral Kolchak in Siberia. The Czech Legion gave its support to the White generals.

The Greens

The national minorities, such as the Georgians, saw an opportunity to establish their independence from Russia. If the Bolsheviks were weak and could be attacked on many fronts, then independence was a possibility. Those who fought the Bolsheviks as groups seeking independence from Russia were known as the Greens.

Foreign powers

Russia's ex-allies, Britain, France, the USA and Japan, all intervened in the war to support the Whites for several reasons:

- Lenin had withdrawn from the war and signed the Treaty of Brest-Liovsk.
- The Bolsheviks cancelled payments of all loans given by the Allies to Russia.
- Britain, France and the USA feared the spread of communism to their own countries. British troops landed in Murmansk in the north, in support of General Yudenich, while Japanese troops landed in the Far East at Vladivostock. British and French troops also supported General Denikin in the south, while the USA sent arms and supplies to help the Whites.

Source A: Map of the Civil War, 1918–21

Czech troops on top of an armoured train on the Trans-Siberian railway

Tasks

1. Study Source A. Using only the map, give the strengths of the Reds and Whites using this grid.

	Strengths	Weaknesses
Reds		
Whites		

2. Which side would be favourite to win the Civil War? Explain your answer.

3. Explain why a civil war broke out in Russia in 1918. (For guidance on answering this type of question, see page 74.)

Chapter 5 Imposing Bolshevik control, 1917–21

Why did the Bolsheviks win the civil war of 1918–21?

At the start of the war, the Bolshevik (Lenin by this time was using the term Communist) government had to move to Moscow and took desperate protective measures to maintain their power.

At first the civil war did not go well for the Reds. They were attacked on all sides by White armies led by experienced commanders and suffered defeat after defeat in 1918 and early 1919:

- General Yudenich, with British support, attacked from the north-west and threatened Petrograd.
- General Denikin, supported mainly by the French, threatened the south, especially the Ukraine.
- With British support, Admiral Kolchak attacked from the east.

RED STRENGTHS	WHITE WEAKNESSES
The Reds adopted the policy of War Communism (see pages 61–63), which meant that all necessary resources were poured into the army – even if this meant peasants and workers went hungry	The Whites were not united in their approach and operated as separate groups. The death of the tsar also weakened support for the Whites, especially from those who had supported his restoration. Nicholas and his family had been kept prisoner by the Reds in Siberia and, later, at Ekaterinburg in the Urals. However, by July 1918, Admiral Kolchak's White armies were approaching Ekaterinburg. Rather than allow the royal family to fall into the hands of the Whites, the Red Guards took them to a cellar where they were shot at point blank range. In later years, there were claims that one of the tsar's daughters, Anastasia, had survived. This seems very unlikely and, in any case, the claims were made by people who believed they would inherit the **Romanov dynasty** millions.
The Red Army was ably led by Trotsky. Conscription was introduced for men aged 18–40, and Trotsky was given the job of organising the enlarged Red Army. Trotsky's army did not have enough officers and so he cleverly recruited former officers of the tsar's army. There were about 22,000 such officers, who were often blackmailed into fighting for the Bolsheviks. The Red Army eventually had some five million troops	Whites were spread over large areas, whereas the Reds were in a central area with good communications
Peasants would often not support the Whites because they feared that the old tsarist system would be restored – for such people, the Bolsheviks were the lesser of two evils	Morale in the White armies was often low and there were many desertions
The use of the *Cheka* (secret police) terrified ordinary Russians. Those found to have helped the Whites or Greens could expect no mercy. Some estimates put the deaths at the hands of the *Cheka* as high as 50,000 during the civil war. (Estimates for those killed by the Whites are even higher.)	Foreign intervention from Britain, France and the USA was half-hearted and served only to increase support for the Communists

However, in 1919 the tide began to turn, due to the leadership and organisation of Trotsky and the weaknesses and divisions of the Whites, who did not attack simultaneously. By mid-1919 Yudenich was within 48 kilometres of Petrograd. However, his army was defeated by the stubborn resistance of the Red Army led by Trotsky.

In the south, Denikin advanced to within 320 kilometres of Moscow. However, a determined counter-attack by Red forces forced Denikin's army to retreat. In the east, Kolchak's army suffered from internal divisions and differences. For example, the Social Revolutionaries refused to fight with Kolchak. In 1920 Kolchak himself was shot.

The table opposite shows in more detail why the tide turned for the Bolsheviks in 1919.

> **Source A:** A description of the impact of a visit by Trotsky to the front during the civil war. This was written by a member of the Red Army
>
> *The town of Gomel was about to fall into the enemy's hands when Trotsky arrived. Then everything changed and the tide began to turn. Trotsky's arrival meant that the city would not be abandoned. He paid a visit to the front lines and made a speech. We were lifted by the energy he carried wherever a critical situation arose. The situation, which was catastrophic twenty-four hours earlier, had improved by his coming – as though by a miracle.*

> **Source B:** Bolshevik poster showing the Whites as dogs, on leads held by the **Allied Powers**. The dogs are named Denikin, Kolchak and Yudenich

> **Source C:** A selection of Trotsky's orders to the Red Army, 1918
>
> - *Every scoundrel who incites anyone to retreat, to desert, or not fulfil a military order will be shot.*
> - *Every soldier of the Red Army who voluntarily deserts his post will be shot.*
> - *Every soldier who throws away his rifle or sells part of his equipment will be shot.*
> - *Those guilty of harbouring deserters are liable to be shot.*
> - *Houses in which deserters are found are liable to be burned down.*

Tasks

1. Does Source A support the evidence of Source C about the leadership of Trotsky during the civil war? Explain your answer.

2. Study Source B.

a) What message is Source B trying to put across?

b) Why do you think the Bolsheviks used posters such as Source B during the civil war?

3. Working in pairs, produce a concept map showing the reasons for the victory of the Reds during the civil war.

- Begin with the most important reason at 12 o'clock and explain your decision.
- Prioritise the other reasons clockwise so that the least important is last.

4. *Was the leadership of Trotsky the main reason for the Bolshevik victory in the civil war? Explain your answer. You may use the following to help you with your answer.*

- *The leadership of Trotsky*
- *The strengths of the Bolsheviks*
- *White differences*
- *Foreign intervention*

(For guidance on answering this type of question, see page 113.)

Chapter 5 Imposing Bolshevik control, 1917–21

Examination practice

This section provides guidance on how to answer question 1c from Unit 2, which is worth eight marks and is the consequence (effects) question.

Question 1 – consequence (effects)
Explain the effects of the Treaty of Brest-Litovsk on Russia in 1918. (8 marks)

How to answer
- Underline key points in the question. Doing this will ensure that you focus sharply on what the question wants you to write about.
- Begin each paragraph by stating the effect and then give a fully developed statement about each effect. One developed effect is worth three marks.
- Make links between each effect.
- Aim to write about at least two effects. Two developed and linked effects will achieve the maximum score (eight marks).

The diagram on the right gives you further guidance on how to answer this type of question.

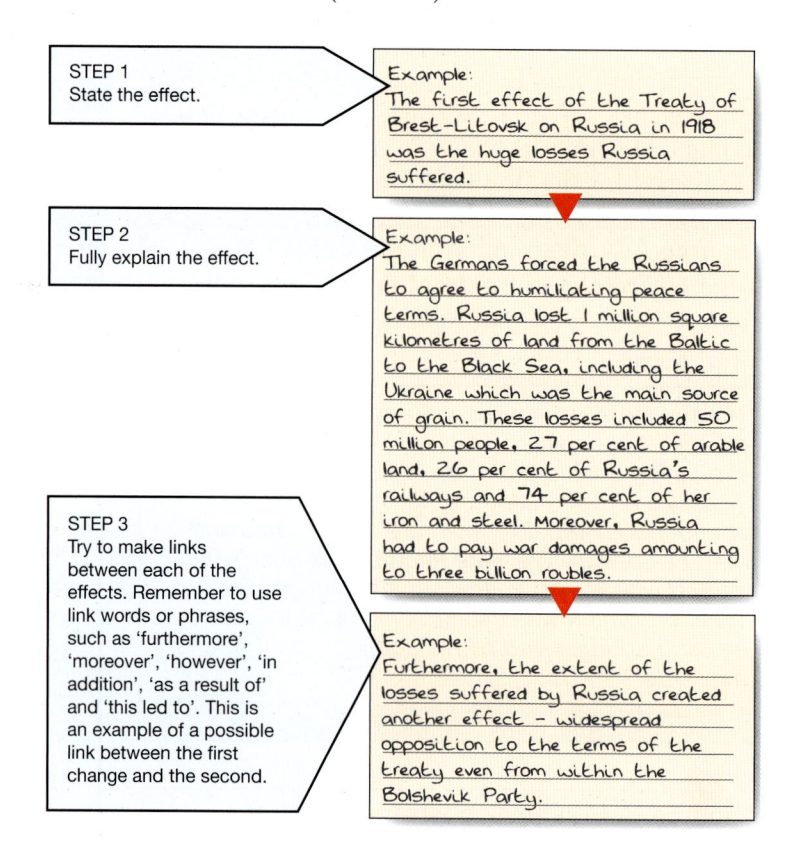

STEP 1 State the effect.

Example: The first effect of the Treaty of Brest-Litovsk on Russia in 1918 was the huge losses Russia suffered.

STEP 2 Fully explain the effect.

Example: The Germans forced the Russians to agree to humiliating peace terms. Russia lost 1 million square kilometres of land from the Baltic to the Black Sea, including the Ukraine which was the main source of grain. These losses included 50 million people, 27 per cent of arable land, 26 per cent of Russia's railways and 74 per cent of her iron and steel. Moreover, Russia had to pay war damages amounting to three billion roubles.

STEP 3 Try to make links between each of the effects. Remember to use link words or phrases, such as 'furthermore', 'moreover', 'however', 'in addition', 'as a result of' and 'this led to'. This is an example of a possible link between the first change and the second.

Example: Furthermore, the extent of the losses suffered by Russia created another effect – widespread opposition to the terms of the treaty even from within the Bolshevik Party.

STEP 4 Fully explain the effect.

STEP 5 If you can discuss one or two other effects then go back to Step 3.

Have a go yourself

Question 2 – consequence (effects)

Explain the effects of the early Bolshevik decrees on the people of Russia in 1917–18. (8 marks)

Now have a go yourself

Try answering question 2 using the steps shown for question 1. Remember to:

- write about at least two effects
- fully explain each effect.

6 Creating a new society, 1918–24

Source A: A starving peasant family during the famine, 1921

Task

1. Prepare a text message to a friend describing what you can see in Source A. Remember you are limited to 160 letters.

2. What does Source A suggest about Russia in 1921?

Within months of seizing power, Lenin introduced War Communism as a method of controlling the economy as well as supplying the needs of the Red Army during the civil war. This proved extremely unpopular with the peasants and industrial workers and seriously undermined the popularity of the Bolshevik regime. This was shown by the Kronstadt Mutiny of 1921, which prompted the end of War Communism, which was replaced by the **New Economic Policy** (NEP). The NEP included elements of capitalism, which upset some of the Bolshevik Party faithful.

This chapter will answer the following questions:

- Why was there opposition to War Communism?
- Why was there a mutiny at Kronstadt?
- What was the New Economic Policy?
- What were the effects of the New Economic Policy?

Examination skills
This chapter provides an opportunity to practise some of the question types from Unit 2.

Why was there opposition to War Communism?

The measures that Lenin and the Communists took to keep the army supplied during the civil war became known as War Communism. War Communism was not one particular law passed by the Bolsheviks. It was a whole series of laws or measures by which the government took control of the economy. It was introduced for several reasons:

Economic	Social
The peasants wanted to keep the land they had been given but were unwilling to sell the food they grew. Lenin wanted to control the supply of food for the towns.	There were severe shortages of food and other basic necessities in Russia. Prices had risen rapidly and there was inflation.
Political	**Military**
The policy followed the Communist idea of central control and direction of the economy.	The Bolsheviks had to guarantee supplies for the huge Red Army during the civil war against the Whites.

Lenin set up the Supreme Council of National Economy *(Vesenkha)* to create a planned economy and a fair society. By the middle of 1918, War Communism meant that the government controlled every aspect of economic life.

The main features of War Communism were:
- Rationing of food in cities was to be strictly applied during food shortages.
- Private trading was banned. Peasants could no longer sell their surplus food for profit but had to give it to the government. Lenin ordered squads into the countryside to seize food if peasants proved unwilling to surrender their produce.
- Factories with more than ten workers were nationalised. This meant that the state now owned the factories. *Vesenkha* decided how much was to be produced in each industry. Workers were under government control and could be told where to work.
- Rapid inflation, which left money valueless. People had to barter, which meant exchanging goods rather than using money.

In theory, Lenin's decision to introduce War Communism was sound, but practically it was flawed. Both workers and peasants objected to it and, as a result, productivity fell (see Source A).

> **Source A:** Industrial and agricultural output in Russia, 1913 and 1921
>
> | Output in million of tonnes | 1913 | 1921 |
> |---|---|---|
> | Grain | 80 | 37.6 |
> | Sugar | 1.3 | 0.05 |
> | Coal | 29 | 9 |
> | Iron | 4.2 | 0.1 |
> | Steel | 4.3 | 0.2 |
> | Oil | 9.2 | 3.8 |
> | Electricity (in million kWh) | 2039 | 520 |

> **Source B:** From *Memoirs of a Revolutionary* by V. Serge, 1945. Here he is writing about food **requisitioning**
>
> *Groups which were sent into the countryside to obtain grain by requisition might be driven away by the peasants with pitchforks. Savage peasants would slit open a Commissar's belly, pack it with grain, and leave him by the roadside as a lesson to all.*

Source C: A White Russian poster of 1919, depicting food requisitioning

Source D: Starving Russian peasants trading in human flesh during the civil war

Food shortages

War Communism was successful on one level because it supplied the Red Army with food and enabled the victory over the Whites. However, the policy failed to create the **utopian communist state** Lenin hoped for. Peasants did not respond well to the idea of giving up produce to the state, and so they grew less and bred fewer animals. The resulting food shortage in 1920 developed into a famine in 1921. It has been estimated that about seven million people died during the famine. There had to be international aid for Russia in the crisis.

A group called Workers' Opposition was formed to press for changes to the policy. One of the group's calls was for 'Soviets without Communists'.

Source E: An eyewitness account by a British refugee from Petrograd, 1918

It is a common occurrence when a horse falls down in the street for the people to cut off the flesh of the animal the moment it has breathed its last. Another way of getting food was by buying it at excessive prices from members of the Red Guard who are well fed.

Tasks

1. *Explain why the Bolsheviks introduced a policy of War Communism.* (For guidance on answering this type of question, see page 74.)

2. *Study Source C. What is the message of the poster?*

3. *Work in pairs. You live in Russia in 1920 and are an opponent of War Communism.*

- Using evidence from Sources B, C D, and E write a letter to Pravda, *the official government newspaper, criticising the policy.*
- Write a reply to be published in Pravda *on behalf of the Bolshevik government.*

Why was there a mutiny at Kronstadt?

The photograph below shows the greatest challenge for Lenin and Trotsky over War Communism, the Kronstadt Naval Rebellion in 1921. Thousands of sailors protested at events in Russia and objected, like the Workers' Opposition, to the way the Communist Party (the Bolsheviks were now called Communists) was taking power away from the soviets.

A photograph showing dead Kronstadt mutineers, surrounded by their grievances

- Terror and despotism have crushed the life born in the October Revolution
- Those who dare to say the truth are imprisoned to suffer the torture cells of the Cheka
- The Revolution is dead. The Bolshevik myth must be destroyed
- Dictatorship is trampling the masses underfoot
- The worker, instead of becoming master of the factory, has become a slave

The Bolshevik reaction

Lenin wanted no opposition and decided to stop the protests. Trotsky had to use the Red Army to put down the rebellion and 20,000 men were killed or wounded in the fighting. The surviving rebels were either executed by the *Cheka* or put in a *gulag*. For other opponents, the end of the rebellion meant the end of any hope of removing the Communists. Lenin realised he had to change the policy – for him, Kronstadt was the 'flash that lit up reality'. In March 1921, Lenin abandoned War Communism and introduced the New Economic Policy in its place.

Source A: What the Kronstadt sailors demanded

- Because the present Soviets do not express the will of the workers and peasants, new elections should be held.
- Freedom of speech and press to be granted to workers and peasants.
- Also freedom of assembly and of trade unions and peasants' associations.
- All political prisoners belonging to Socialist parties to be set free.

Tasks

1. Study Source A and the text surrounding the photograph, which gives the grievances of the Kronstadt sailors. Using evidence from Lenin's government of 1918–21, do you think their grievances were justified?

2. Produce a newspaper headline for *Pravda*, the official government newspaper, about the rebellion.

3. Why do you think the mutiny was crushed so quickly and with such brutality?

What was the New Economic Policy?

Reasons for the NEP

The New Economic Policy (NEP) was intended by Lenin primarily to meet Russia's urgent need for food. If the peasants could not be forced, then they must be persuaded. He also felt that the new policy would give Russia some breathing space after a period of almost eight years' war. There were some Communists who felt that they were betraying the revolution by reverting back to capitalism.

The NEP said that:
- peasants would still have to give a fixed amount of grain to the government, but they could sell their surplus for profit again
- peasants who increased their food production would pay less tax
- factories with less than 20 workers would be given back to their owners and consumer goods could be produced and sold for profit
- people could use money again and a new rouble was introduced
- key industries, such as coal and steel, still remained under state control.

The NEP also included the electrification of Russia. Lenin was convinced that electrical power was the key to economic growth. A network of power stations was established in the years after 1921. NEP also encouraged foreign trade with countries such as Britain because Lenin believed that the move towards capitalism would finally destroy communism in Russia. Over the next few years, there were large-scale exchanges of Western industrial goods for Russian oil and wheat.

Source A: Poster promoting the electrification of Russia

Source A: From a speech by Lenin to party members in 1921

We are now retreating, going back as it were, but we are doing this so as to retreat first and then run and leap forward more vigorously. We retreated on this one condition alone when we introduced our New Economic Policy ... so as to begin a more determined offensive after the retreat.

Tasks

1. What reason does Lenin suggest in Source A for the introduction of the NEP?

2. *Explain why the NEP was introduced.* (For guidance on answering this type of question, see page 74.)

Chapter 6 Creating a new society, 1918–24

What were the effects of the New Economic Policy?

Debate about the NEP continued throughout its existence. However, when Lenin died in 1924, the debate was set to become ever fiercer within the Communist Party.

Trotsky described the New Economic Policy as the 'first sign of the degeneration of Bolshevism'. One rumour had it that the letters NEP stood for 'New Exploitation of the Proletariat'. Those who criticised the NEP said that a new class was created – '**NEPMEN**'. This term was applied to those who stood to gain from the capitalism permitted under the new policy: these were the *kulaks*, the retailers and the small manufacturers. It was said that greed and selfishness were returning to Russia. However, there was clearly an economic recovery under the New Economic Policy, as Source A indicates.

> **Source B:** From the book *From Lenin to Stalin* by Victor Serge, a former Communist. This was written in 1937. Here he was attacking the NEP
>
> *In just a few years, the NEP restored to Russia an aspect of prosperity. But to many of us this prosperity was sometimes distasteful ... we felt ourselves sinking into the mire – paralysed, corrupted ... There was gambling, drunkenness and all the old filth of former times ... Classes were re-born under our eyes ... There was a growing gap between the prosperity of the few and the misery of the many.*

Source A: Agricultural and industrial recovery during the New Economic Policy

	1921	1922	1923	1924	1925
Agriculture					
Sown area (million hectares)	90.3	77.7	91.7	98.1	104.3
Grain harvest (million tonnes)	37.6	50.3	56.6	51.4	72.5
Industry					
Coal (million tonnes)	8.9	9.5	13.7	16.1	18.1
Steel (thousand tonnes)	183	39	709	1140	2135
Finished cloth (million metres)	105	349	691	963	1688
Value of factory output (million roubles)	2004	2619	4005	4660	7739
Electricity (million Kwhs)	520	775	1146	1562	2925
Rail freight carried (million tonnes)	39.4	39.9	58.0	67.5	83.4
Average monthly wage of urban worker (in roubles)	10.2	12.2	15.9	20.8	25.2

Source C: Written in the 1980s by Leonid Orlov, a Bolshevik supporter

There wasn't a scrap of food in the country. We were down to a quarter of a pound (114g) of bread per person. Then suddenly they announced the NEP. Cafes started opening as well as restaurants. Factories went back into private hands. It was capitalism. In my eyes what was happening was the very thing I'd struggled against.

Source D: From a history of Russia written in 1996

By 1921 famine had broken out. Industrial production was down to one seventh of the 1913 level. It is estimated that 3.5 million people died from typhoid alone. With the economy in ruins, inflation out of control and the country in the grip of famine, the peasants called for the overthrow of Communism.

Source E: Photograph of Nepmen in Smolensk market, 1921

Tasks

1. Explain why Trotsky and Serge opposed the New Economic Policy.

2. Study Sources A, B, C and E. Which sources suggest that:

   a) The NEP was a success

   b) The NEP was a failure?

3. Which of the following statements best sums up the NEP? Give reasons for your choice.

   - The NEP was a popular and successful policy
   - The NEP was an unpopular but successful policy
   - The NEP was an unpopular and unsuccessful policy.

Examination practice

Question 1 – source inference

What can you learn from Source D about Russia in 1921? (4 marks)
(Remember how to answer this type of question? For further guidance, see page 24.)

Question 2 – describe

Describe the key features of the policy of War Communism. (6 marks)
(Remember how to answer this type of question? For further guidance, see page 39.)

Question 3 – causation

Explain why there was a rebellion by the sailors at Kronstadt in 1921. (8 marks)
(For guidance on answering this type of question, see page 74.)

Question 4 – consequence (effects)

Explain the effects of the New Economic Policy on the Soviet Union in the years 1921–24. (8 marks)
(Remember how to answer this type of question? For further guidance, see page 60.)

Chapter 6 Creating a new society, 1918–24

Key Topic 3: The nature of Stalin's dictatorship, 1924–39

Tasks

1. Study Source A. Who is circled in the centre? (Answer on page 126.)
2. Can you find Stalin? (Answer on page 126.)
3. What does this suggest about his chances of succeeding Lenin?

Source A: A photo-montage, which shows the leading Bolsheviks in the mid-1920s

This key topic examines the struggle for power in the years after Lenin's death and how Stalin was able to overcome his rivals, especially Trotsky, and win the leadership contest by 1928. This is followed by an explanation of Stalin's **purges** of the 1930s, especially the reasons for the purges, which groups were purged, the effects of the purges on Soviet society and the importance of the '**show trials**'.

The last chapter in this key topic examines two key elements within Stalin's dictatorship, propaganda and **censorship**. This includes the promotion of Stalin himself, through the cult of Stalin, and control of culture, through social realism and education, as well as the importance of the 1936 Constitution.

Each chapter explains a key issue and examines important lines of enquiry as outlined below:

Chapter 7 The struggle for power, 1924-28 (pages 69–74)

- Who was Stalin?
- Who were Stalin's leadership rivals?
- How did Stalin remove his rivals?
- Why did Stalin win the leadership contest?

Chapter 8 The purges of the 1930s, (pages 75–84)

- What were the purges?
- Why did Stalin introduce the purges?
- How were the purges carried out?
- What were the 'show trials'?
- What were the effects of the purges?

Chapter 9 Propaganda and censorship (pages 85–93)

- What was the cult of Stalin?
- How was culture controlled by Stalin?
- How did Stalin control religion?
- What changes were made in education?
- What was the new constitution of 1936?

7 The struggle for power, 1924–28

Source A: A Red Army officer writing in 1992 about Trotsky and Stalin

*More than anything we were frightened of Trotsky seizing power, though we now know that was not the main problem. In those days Stalin was an unknown figure to us. I worked in the **Kremlin** and I didn't know who Stalin was, and I was a Red Commander.*

Source B: A Communist Pary member, Iosti Itskov, talking about Stalin in later years

He tried to stay in the shadows. He was a man whose aim was very clear, but you could not tell how he was going to accomplish it. He accomplished it in the most cunning way. And he allowed nothing to get in his way.

Tasks

1. What does Source A suggest about Trotsky and Stalin?
2. Does Source B support the views about Stalin expressed in Source A?

Lenin died in 1924. There followed a four-year struggle to decide who would succeed him as leader. Trotsky was the favourite due to his leadership of the **Red Army** and his achievements in the years 1917–24. Stalin was very much the outsider. He was not well known outside political circles, nor did he have Trotsky's intellect and experience. Nevertheless, through a combination of his own shrewdness and Trotsky's over-confidence and weaknesses, Stalin had, by 1928, won the leadership contest.

This chapter will answer the following questions:

- Who was Stalin?
- Who were Stalin's leadership rivals?
- How did Stalin remove his rivals?
- Why did Stalin win the leadership contest?

Examination skills

This chapter gives guidance on question 1d from Unit 2. This question, which is worth eight marks, is a causation question.

Who was Stalin?

Stalin was born in 1879 in the state of Georgia, the son of a bootmaker. His real name was Joseph Djugashvili. He was from a poor background and had a harsh upbringing. Nevertheless, his mother was determined that he should do well and she worked hard to pay for his education. Indeed, he gained a scholarship to a college for training priests in Tiblisi. However, he lost interest in God when he discovered **Marxism** and, in 1899, was expelled from the college.

He greatly admired the writings of Lenin and became a member of the **Bolshevik** Party (see page 16), taking the name of Stalin, meaning 'Man of Steel'. In the period after 1902, he became an active revolutionary, taking part in over 1000 raids to seize money for the party. He was arrested and exiled to Siberia eight times, escaping on seven occasions.

He was freed from exile in 1917 and returned to Petrograd to become editor of *Pravda*, the Bolshevik newspaper. The evidence suggests he played little role in the **Bolshevik Revolution** of 1917 (see page 42). Nevertheless, he was made **Commissar of Nationalities** in Lenin's government and crushed a rebellion in his own state of Georgia with great brutality. In 1922, he was given what was regarded as the most boring and dull of jobs, General Secretary of the Bolshevik Party, responsible for the day-to-day running of the Party and the appointment and dismissal of key members.

Task

Draw up a brief curriculum vitae for Stalin up to 1922. You could use the headings in the example below, or design your own.

A photograph of Stalin after his arrest in 1902

Curriculum Vitae

Name: Joseph Stalin

Skills

Education

Work experience

Interests

Key Topic 3 The nature of Stalin's dictatorship, 1924–39

Who were Stalin's leadership rivals?

After Lenin's death in 1924 there was a struggle for power in Russia. There were five possible candidates to succeed Lenin. If you had been able to place a bet on the successful candidate, the odds would have read something like those in the betting shop below. By 1928 Stalin had emerged as leader. Why was the rank outsider successful?

Task

Apart from Trotsky, which of the other three was the greatest threat to Stalin? Give reasons for your answer.

BETTING SHOP

Who will succeed Lenin?

Leon Trotsky

2/1 favourite

He had organised the successful Bolshevik Revolution of 1917 and led the Red Army to victory in the Russian Civil War. He was very intelligent and Lenin's choice as his successor.

Lev Kamenev

20/1 outsider

Although he angered Lenin by opposing the Bolshevik Revolution of 1917, he was made the leader of the Bolshevik Party in Moscow.

Joseph Stalin

100/1 rank outsider

He had played little part in the Bolshevik Revolution of 1917. Moreover Lenin, himself, did not want Stalin to succeed him and, in his last testament, tried to warn other leading Bolsheviks about him (see Source A on page 72).

Gregory Zinoviev

15/1 outsider

He had helped Lenin to set up the Bolshevik Party in 1903. During Lenin's government he was made the Bolshevik Party boss in Petrograd and was head of the **Comintern**, the organisation through which Soviet Russia tried to bring about Communist revolutions in other countries.

Nikolai Bukharin

25/1 outsider

He was a leading Bolshevik who had opposed the Treaty of Brest-Litovsk by which Russia lost much land to Germany in March 1918. He was a firm supporter of Lenin's **New Economic Policy**.

Chapter 7 The struggle for power, 1924–28

How did Stalin remove his rivals?

Lenin's Will and Testament

Source A: Lenin's views on Stalin in his Testament, 1923

Comrade Stalin, having become Secretary, has unlimited authority concentrated in his hands and I am not sure whether he will be capable of using that authority with sufficient caution. Comrade Trotsky, on the other hand, is perhaps the most capable man in the present Committee. Stalin is too rude and this fault is not acceptable in the office of Secretary. Therefore I propose to comrades that they find a way of removing Stalin from his post.

Lenin's **Testament** meant that Stalin had little or no chance of winning the leadership contest. However, he cunningly persuaded other members of the Central Committee, especially Kamenev and Zinoviev, to keep the Testament secret for the sake of Party unity and because it also criticised them.

Lenin's Funeral

Stalin successfully presented himself as Lenin's close follower. For example, Stalin appeared as the chief mourner at Lenin's funeral, while Trotsky was conspicuous by his absence. Trotsky was ill and Stalin tricked him into believing the funeral was the following day. Trotsky was seen as arrogant and disrespectful of Lenin because he could not be bothered to turn up for his funeral.

'Socialism in One Country'

Stalin worked closely with Zinoviev and Kamenev and, in 1925, they forced Trotsky to resign as Commissar of War. He no longer had control of the Red Army. Moreover, Stalin packed the Congress of Soviets with his supporters to gain support for his policy of '**Socialism** in One Country'.

Zinoviev and Kamenev

In 1926 Stalin worked with Bukharin and the **right wing** of the Communist Party, who supported his idea of 'Socialism in One Country', against Zinoviev, Kamenev and Trotsky who, in 1927, were all expelled from the Party.

Bukharin

By 1928 Stalin felt strong enough to turn against Bukharin and his supporters on the right wing of the Party. They supported the NEP, which Stalin wanted to abandon and replace with a new policy of industrial expansion. In 1929, Bukharin was forced to resign.

Assassination of Trotsky

In 1929 Trotsky was expelled from the Soviet Union. In 1937 he settled in Mexico, where he wrote many articles attacking Stalin, who saw him as a major threat. On 20 August 1940 Trotsky was assassinated by a hired hitman, Ramon Mercador, who put an ice-pick through his head.

Why did Stalin win the leadership contest?

Stalin's success was due to a combination of his own strengths and the weaknesses of his rivals, especially Trotsky.

Strengths of Stalin	Weaknesses of Trotsky
• Stalin held the key role of General Secretary in the Communist Party. He used this position to appoint officials who supported him and he removed known supporters of Trotsky in order to build up a power base. He soon commanded the support of most Party officials. • He built up an image of someone who had been close to Lenin, and was therefore his natural successor. He was the chief mourner at Lenin's funeral and made a speech praising him. He had photos published showing him at Lenin's side. • Stalin cleverly played off his rivals against each other. He knew that Kamenev and Zinoviev feared Trotsky and used their support to remove him. He then allied himself with Bukharin and the right wing of the Party to remove Kamenev and Zinoviev. • He promoted 'Socialism in One Country', which won popular support within the Communist Party because it suggested that the Soviet Union should concentrate on securing communism at home before it supported revolutions abroad.	• Trotsky was seen by many Party members as an outsider, partly because he was Jewish, but also because, from 1903 to 1917, he had been a **Menshevik**, only changing to the Bolshevik Party shortly before the October Revolution. • He made a series of tactical mistakes and allowed himself to be out-manoeuvred by Stalin. As leader of the Red Army, he had the power to remove his leader. Instead, he resigned as commander. In addition, he was not prepared to canvas support from his colleagues or rank-and-file members of the Communist Party. • Trotsky promoted world revolution. He wanted the Soviet Union to support communist revolutions in other countries. However, most Russians preferred to concentrate their resources and energy on fully establishing communism in the Soviet Union ('Socialism in One Country').

Source B: A photograph showing a demonstration against Trotsky

Tasks

1. Why might Stalin have encouraged the demonstration shown in Source B?

2. Work in pairs. One of you is Stalin and the other Trotsky. You are to be interviewed by the **Politburo** members for the job of Party leader. Prepare a presentation/speech for your candidate. Remember to stress your strengths and the weaknesses of your opponent.

3. Lenin has just died and you are a friend and adviser to Trotsky. Write a letter to Trotsky giving him advice on how he can win the leadership contest.

Examination practice

This section provides guidance on how to answer question 1d from Unit 2, which is worth eight marks.

Question 1 – causation
Explain why Stalin was able to win the leadership contest in the years 1924–28.
(8 marks)

How to answer

- Underline key points in the question – for example, the key theme, dates and the command word.

- Ensure that you focus on causes. Begin each paragraph by stating a cause and then fully develop each cause you give. Use precise knowledge which will impress the examiner, such as specific dates, statistics and names.

- Make links between one cause and the next. Use link words or phrases, such as 'furthermore', 'moreover', 'however', 'in addition', 'as a result of', and 'this led to'.

- Aim to write about at least two causes. Two developed causes will achieve the maximum score (eight marks).

The diagram on the right gives you further guidance on how to answer this type of question.

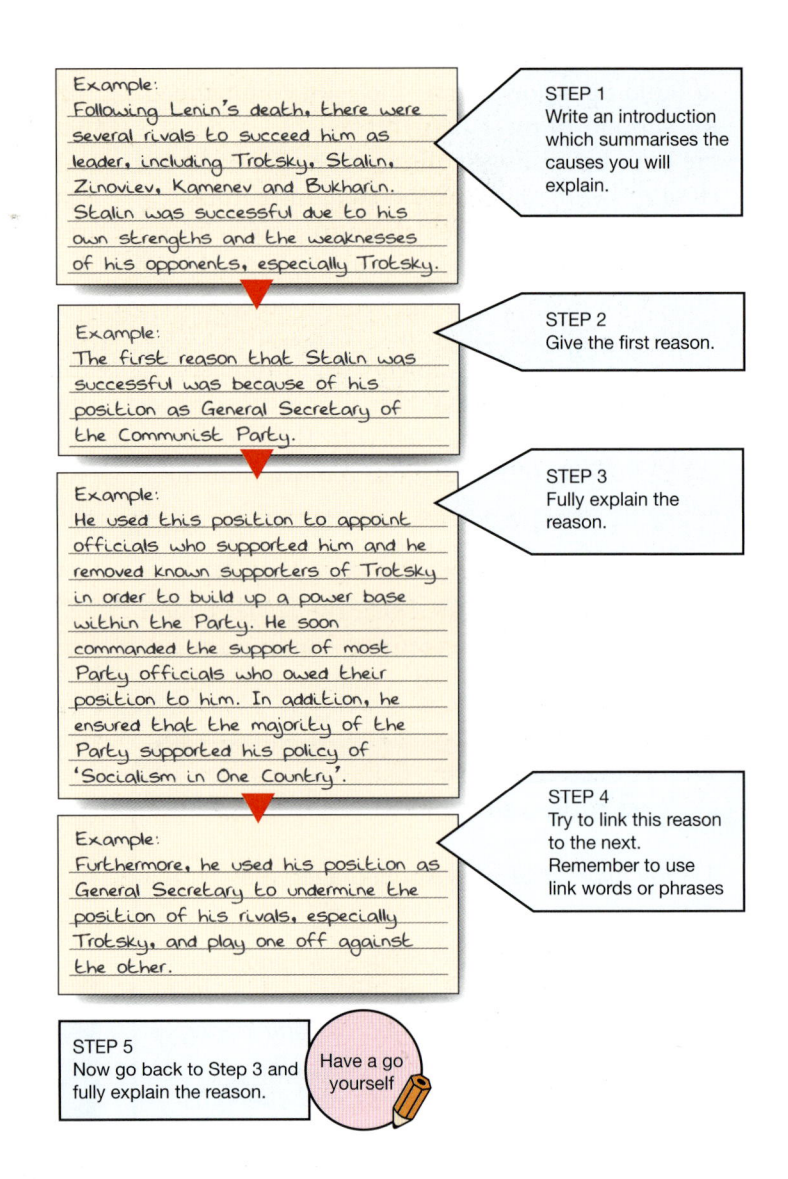

Example:
Following Lenin's death, there were several rivals to succeed him as leader, including Trotsky, Stalin, Zinoviev, Kamenev and Bukharin. Stalin was successful due to his own strengths and the weaknesses of his opponents, especially Trotsky.

STEP 1 Write an introduction which summarises the causes you will explain.

Example:
The first reason that Stalin was successful was because of his position as General Secretary of the Communist Party.

STEP 2 Give the first reason.

Example:
He used this position to appoint officials who supported him and he removed known supporters of Trotsky in order to build up a power base within the Party. He soon commanded the support of most Party officials who owed their position to him. In addition, he ensured that the majority of the Party supported his policy of 'Socialism in One Country'.

STEP 3 Fully explain the reason.

Example:
Furthermore, he used his position as General Secretary to undermine the position of his rivals, especially Trotsky, and play one off against the other.

STEP 4 Try to link this reason to the next. Remember to use link words or phrases.

STEP 5 Now go back to Step 3 and fully explain the reason.

Have a go yourself

8 The purges of the 1930s

This shows Stalin (middle) next to Yezhov (right)

This shows the same photograph a few years later

Tasks

Study the two photographs.

1. What is different about the second picture?
2. What do you think might have happened in the meantime? (Answer on page 126.)

In the 1930s, Stalin established probably the most effective and ruthless dictatorship of the twentieth century. This involved not only a systematic programme of propaganda, culminating in the 'Cult of Stalin', but the removal of any potential threats to his position, which in turn led to the death of millions of people in the Soviet Union.

This chapter will answer the following questions:

- What were the purges?
- Why did Stalin introduce the purges?
- How were the purges carried out?
- What were the 'show trials'?
- What were the effects of the purges?

Examination skills

This chapter gives guidance on question 2a from Unit 2. This question, which is worth eight marks, can be one of two types: either a change, or an 'explain how' question. This chapter looks at the change question.

What were the purges?

In the 1930s, Stalin embarked on a series of **purges,** which led to the death and imprisonment of millions of Soviet people. No one was immune.

Stalin purged anyone who held up, criticised or opposed his plans for **collectivisation** and **industrialisation** (see page 97). Most of the accused were deported or imprisoned. Some were shot. The first victims were managers and workers accused of wrecking the first **Five-Year Plan**, *kulaks* accused of opposition to collectivisation and ordinary Party members accused of incorrect attitudes. The following flow diagram shows the key features of Stalin's purges.

1928
55 engineers from Shakhty mines in Donbas were put on trial accused of sabotage, with five shot and 49 imprisoned.

1932
Ryutin, a senior member of the Communist Party, criticised Stalin's economic policies. A furious Stalin had Ryutin and his supporters arrested and put on trial. Ryutin was expelled from the Party and sent into exile.

1934
Following the murder of Kirov (see page 89), thousands of Communist Party members were arrested, 40,000 in Leningrad alone.

1935
Senior Communists were arrested: 1108 out of 1966 delegates to the 17th Congress; 98 out of 139 members of the Central Committee. Party branches were told to root out anyone who had supported Trotsky. Thousands were denounced and expelled.

1936
The 'show trials' of the 'old Bolsheviks' (see page 81). Zinoviev, Kamenev and other Left Opposition leaders were arrested and confessed to plotting after **NKVD** (secret police) torture and brainwashing.

Source A: A photograph of 1936 from an American newspaper showing the leading Bolsheviks purged by Stalin

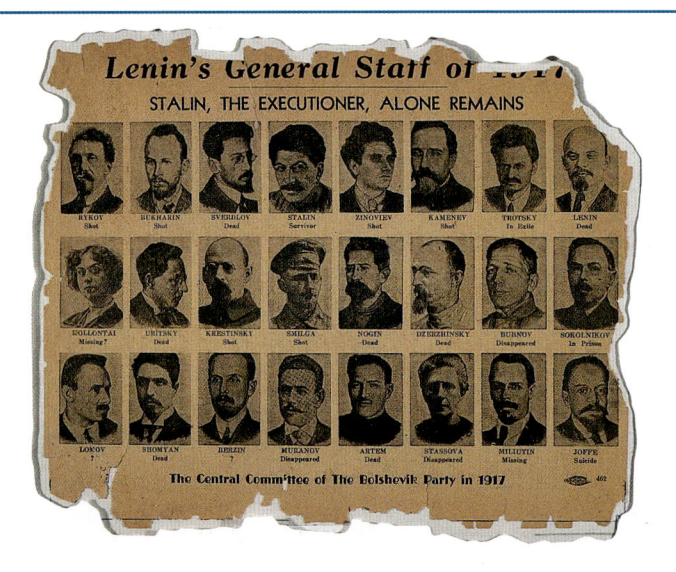

1937
Stalin was determined to remove any possible opposition in the Red Army and ensure total obedience. The Commander-in-Chief, Marshall Tukhachevsky, and seven other generals were arrested and shot. Tukhachevsky had had serious disagreements with Stalin during the Russian Civil War of 1918–21. In addition, the commanders of the armed forces could be powerful enough to overthrow Stalin. By 1941, almost 90 per cent of all Soviet generals had been purged.

1938
By this year, almost every party and state leader in every one of the Soviet republics had been purged. Stalin called a halt to the purges, which were getting out of hand. He blamed the secret police, which itself was purged to remove all knowledge of what happened. This purge included Yezhov (see page 80).

1940
Trotsky was murdered by one of Stalin's agents in Mexico in 1940.

Source C: A French cartoon of the late 1930s, which shows Stalin controlling the purges

Source B: Popular stories/jokes used during the purges

Question: Why do the secret police always travel in threes?
Answer: One can read, one can write and the third is there to keep an eye on the two intellectuals.

A flock of sheep was stopped by frontier guards at the border with Finland.
'Why do you want to leave Russia?' the guards asked.
'It's the NKVD,' replied the terrified sheep. 'Beria (Chief of Police) has ordered them to arrest elephants.'
'But you're not elephants!' the guards exclaimed.
'Yes,' said the sheep, 'but try telling that to the NKVD.'

A man, sitting in his flat, heard a loud knock at the door.
'Who is it?' he asked anxiously.
'It is the Angel of Death.'
'Phew!' the man exclaimed. 'For a moment I thought it was the secret police!'

Tasks

1. What does Source A tell you about Stalin and the purges?

2. Look at Source B on jokes made during the purges. Can you make up your own joke? (One possibility is a 'knock, knock' type joke.)

3. Study Source C.
a) What message is the cartoonist trying to get across?
b) How does the cartoonist achieve this?

4. Describe the key features of the purges of the 1930s. (Remember how to answer this type of question? For further guidance, see page 39.)

Chapter 8 The purges of the 1930s

Why did Stalin introduce the purges?

Why did Stalin introduce the purges?

There was no single reason why Stalin introduced the purges. Indeed, a number of theories and explanations have been given.

1. Threats to his position

Stalin was concerned that his enemies were plotting to overthrow him. His real motive may have been to destroy any men who might form an alternative government – especially the 'Old Bolsheviks'.

> **Source A:** Bukharin speaking in 1936
>
> Stalin is convinced that he is greater than everyone else. If someone speaks better than he does, that man is for it. Stalin will not let him live, because that man is a constant reminder that he, Stalin, is not the first and best. He is not a man but a devil.

2. Stalin not totally responsible

Others believe that once the purges started they had a snowball effect and were difficult to stop. Stalin may have started them but lost control at local level where they were often used by unscrupulous people to get rid of rivals or those in a coveted superior position.

3. Links with economic policies

One theory argues that it was the only way Stalin could get mass forced labour for his industrial projects. The purges were also a convenient way of excusing setbacks. For example, failures to achieve targets under the Five-Year Plans (see page 106) could be blamed on sabotage rather than faults in the Plan.

Stalin was convinced that he was the only person who could transform the Soviet Union into a modern, industrialised country and that it had to be done quickly. He believed that Hitler would attack the USSR and that it would lose the war if it could not produce enough armaments. Any person who tried to stop him accomplishing this great task was, in Stalin's eyes, a traitor.

Reasons for the purges

4. Persecution complex

Some writers, including British writer C. P. Snow, believe Stalin was suffering from a 'persecution complex' – that he feared everyone was plotting against him. The murder of Kirov is an example of this.

Source B: A Soviet cartoon of 1937 called 'The Murderer's Hygiene'. It shows Trotsky as an executioner washing his hands in blood in a German helmet.

The murder of Kirov

Stalin decided that his popular *Politburo* colleague, Kirov, was a possible rival. Kirov, a leading communist, spoke at the Seventeenth Party Congress in 1934. He criticised Stalin's policy on industrialisation and insisted that it should be slowed down. Kirov's speech was warmly applauded and there was even talk of him replacing Stalin as leader.

He was murdered, probably on Stalin's orders. Stalin claimed the murder was part of a plot against him and the Party. The secret police arrested thousands of Kirov's supporters.

Kirov speaking at the Seventeenth Party Congress, 1934

Source C: Vladimir Alliluyev, Stalin's nephew, wrote in 1990 *Stalin, a Time for Judgement*, and insisted his uncle was not involved with the murder

Stalin had nothing to do with that murder. My mother was with him when they phoned and informed him that Kirov had been murdered. And my mother said to me, neither before nor after it had she ever seen Stalin in the state he was in after receiving that phone call. And Stalin knew full well that the murder would be linked with his name.

Source D: Olga Shatunovskaya, a member of the 1955 commission that inquired into Kirov's death, thought differently

The secret police latched on to the idea that Stalin was dissatisfied after he wrote them a letter saying:

'I am ready for anything now. I hate Kirov.'

And they organised the murder. Of course when Stalin found out that some senior Party members had asked Kirov to become leader, he decided to remove him.

Tasks

1. What does Source A suggest about the reasons for the purges?

2. What is the message of Source B?

3. Does Source D support the evidence of Source C about who was responsible for the murder of Kirov? Explain your answer.

4. Organise the explanations for the purges under the following categories. Do some fall under more than one category? Why might this be the case?

Economic	Political	Psychological

a) Rank order the reasons given for the purges, starting with the most convincing and finishing with the least convincing.

b) Explain your reasons for the first and last in your rank order.

5. Explain why Stalin carried out the purges. (Remember how to answer this type of question? For further guidance, see page 74.)

How were the purges carried out?

The purges were implemented by the secret police and many of those purged ended up in labour camps known as *gulags*.

The secret police

Lenin set up his own secret police known as the *Cheka*, which was renamed the **OGPU** in 1922. In 1934, its name was changed again – to the **NKVD**.

Stalin expanded the secret police and gave it greatly increased powers with the 'decree against terrorist acts', issued after Kirov's murder. This meant they could arrest people without charge or trial and execute them on the spot.

The secret police were sent out at night and were nicknamed the 'black ravens', because they drove round in black cars. They liked to call in the early hours of the morning.

They were assisted by an army of informers. Even children were encouraged to inform on their parents, neighbours and school friends. Informing on others was a way of showing your loyalty, of settling old scores and of getting someone else's more senior job or position.

The NKVD was used by Stalin to hunt down and destroy his opponents and terrorise ordinary people into obedience. People found guilty of opposition or disobedience were sentenced to death, exile or hard labour. The most notorious head of the secret police was Yezhov who was himself purged in 1938.

The labour camps

Victims of the purges were sent to the *gulags*, which were set up in Siberia and the Arctic north. They were run by the secret police. Millions of people were imprisoned and forced to do hard manual work on construction and mining projects. About thirteen million died from cold, hunger and ill-treatment. Living conditions were appalling and food supplies totally inadequate. In 1928, there were around 30,000 prisoners in the labour camps. By 1938, it was around seven million.

Source A: From the *Gulag Archipelago*, written in 1973 by Alexander Solzhenitsyn. He served time in a labour camp for eight years in the 1940s

In 1938 Ivanor Razannik found 140 prisoners in a cell intended for 25 – with toilets so overburdened that prisoners were taken to the toilet only once a day, sometimes at night. He calculated that for weeks at a time there were three persons per square yard of floor space. In this 'kennel' there was neither ventilation nor a window and the prisoners' body heat and breathing raised the temperature to 40 degrees centigrade. Their naked bodies were pressed against one another and they got eczema from one another's sweat. They sat like that for weeks ... and were given neither fresh air nor water – except for gruel and tea in the morning.

Gulag prisoners working on the Belomar Canal in 1931. They were expected to do the basic labouring jobs.

Tasks

1. What was meant by the 'gulags'?

2. Solzhenitsyn was writing about the gulags in a novel. Is Source A still useful as evidence of life in the gulags even though it is fiction? Explain your answer.

What were the 'show trials'?

Source A: A cartoon of the mid-1930s from an American newspaper showing leading Bolsheviks at the show trials

[Cartoon with speech bubbles: "YES, I'M GUILTY!", "SURE, I TRIED TO BETRAY MY COUNTRY.", "OF COURSE I'M A TRAITOR!", "THERE'S NO DOUBT ABOUT MY GUILT."]

The show trials began in 1936. In that year, Stalin began purging the Communist Party of anyone who might oppose him, especially 'Old Bolsheviks', such as Kamenev and Zinoviev. Along with fourteen others, they were accused of organising Kirov's murder and plotting to assassinate Stalin.

The accused were put on trial in full view of the world. They were forced to confess to a whole range of improbable crimes, including a plot to murder Lenin. The confessions were important because they appeared to show that Stalin was right to purge the Communist Party. Trotsky, now in exile, was accused of leading the plotters.

Why did they confess to such crimes?

Such confessions did not help the accused, as they were executed after the trials. They confessed for a number of reasons: first, because they were physically and psychologically tortured by the secret police (see Source B); second, because their families were threatened with imprisonment or death.

Source B: From Evgenia Ginsburg, who was tortured and wrote an account in *Into the Whirlwind* in 1968

They started to work on me again. I was put on the 'conveyor belt'. The interrogators worked in shifts. I didn't. Seven days without sleep or food. Relaxed and fresh, they passed before me as a dream. The object of the 'conveyor' is to wear out the nerves, weaken the body, break resistance, and force the prisoner to sign whatever is required. Others confessed for the sake of their families and some, most especially Bukharin, confessed as a last service to the Communist Party.

Source C: From Fitzroy MacLean, a British diplomat who observed the show trials

The prisoners were charged with every possible crime including high treason, murder, spying and all sorts of sabotage. They were accused of plotting to wreck industry and agriculture, to assassinate Stalin and break up the Soviet Union. Some were accused of betraying the Soviet cause even before the Bolshevik Revolution of 1917. One after another, using the same words, they admitted their guilt. And yet what they said seemed to bear no relation to reality.

Tasks

1. What point is the cartoonist trying to get across in Source A?
2. How does the cartoonist achieve this?
3. Does Source B support the evidence of Source C about the show trials?
4. Describe the key features of the show trials. (Remember how to answer this type of question? For further guidance, see page 39.)

What were the effects of the purges?

The purges did ensure total control under Stalin, with the removal of any potential rivals to his leadership. However, they had a devastating effect on the Soviet Union.

The human cost was enormous. It is impossible to know how many were killed or imprisoned. However, in 1988 the **KGB** – the name for the secret police at that time – allowed some NKVD files to be examined. This revealed the following figures for 1937–38:

FATE	NUMBER OF PEOPLE
Executed	1 million
Died in labour camps	2 million
In prison, late 1938	1 million
In labour camps, late 1938	8 million

Source A: A photograph of a mass grave at Cheliabinsk in the Urals taken in 1938

The USSR was seriously weakened with the loss of its senior officers in the army and navy. This almost led to defeat in 1941 when Hitler's armies invaded.

The purges undermined much of Stalin's earlier work on building up industry (see page 106). Able scientists, administrators and engineers were arrested, executed or imprisoned, which affected the quality of what was being produced.

Every part of Russia was affected. No village, no home, not even Stalin's own family could escape. His cousins and in-laws were victims of **the Terror**. Anyone could receive a knock on the door in the middle of the night and be dragged away by the secret police.

No one felt secure. Some people took advantage to denounce neighbours or workmates and get their jobs. All trust disappeared. Eventually, the secret police had files on half the urban population in the Soviet Union.

Many were unfairly expelled from the Communist Party. This often had cruel consequences. Without the Party card, it was impossible to get a job. This punished the whole family. When both parents of one 13-year-old girl were arrested she was forced to live on the streets. In order to survive she had to tell the Young Pioneers (see page 91) that her parents were spies and deserved to be shot.

Source B: Osip Mandelstam, a poet who was arrested in 1934, on the effects of the purges

Everybody seemed intent on his daily round and went smilingly about the business of carrying out his instructions. It was essential to smile – if you didn't it meant you were afraid or discontented. This nobody could afford to admit – if you were afraid, you must have a bad conscience. Everyone had to strut around wearing a cheerful expression as though to say:

'What's going on is no concern of mine. I have important work to do and I'm terribly busy. I am trying to do my best for the State, so do not get in my way.'

Source C: A French cartoon published in the late 1930s. The caption reads 'Visit the Pyramids of the USSR'

Tasks

1. Study Source A. Why do you think that the bodies were buried in mass graves?

2. What does Source B suggest about the effects of the purges on everyday life?

3. What message is the cartoonist trying to get across in Source C?

4. Using a concept map, show the effects of the purges. You may wish to use the following categories – military, political, economic, social and psychological.

- Using a different colour, show on your concept map any links between the effects.
- Explain at least one of your links.

An example of how you could start your concept map is given below.

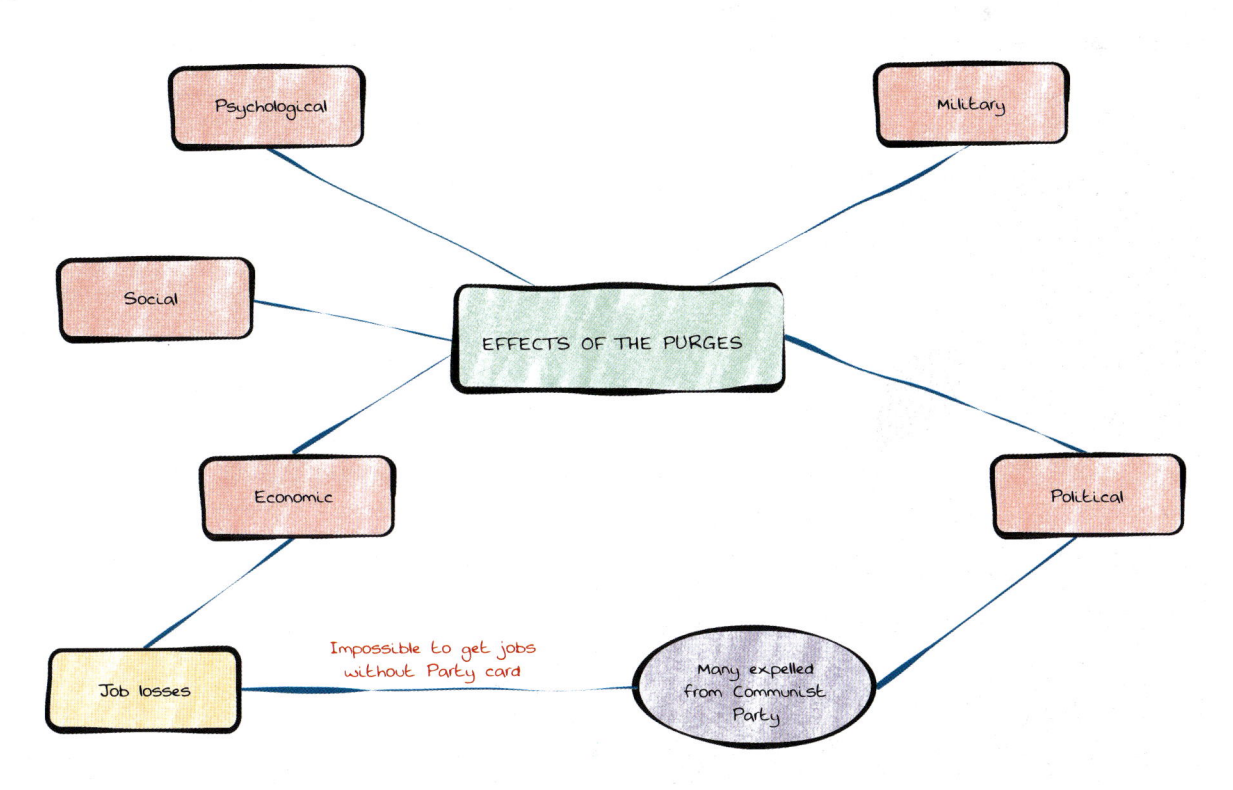

The subject nationalities

Stalin was from Georgia, an area that had long wanted self-government and even independence. Unlike Lenin, however, Stalin had no sympathy with these national groups. In the 1930s, a policy of '**Russification**' attempted to impose Russian culture on the USSR. Russian became compulsory in schools and key jobs went to Russians. Army recruits were sent away from their homelands and forced to mix with other ethnic groups. Many who opposed this were purged.

Chapter 8 The purges of the 1930s

Examination practice

This section provides guidance on how to answer question 2a from Unit 2, which is worth eight marks. This is the change or 'explain how' question.

Question 1 – change
Explain how the purges changed life in the Soviet Union in the 1930s. (8 marks)

How to answer
- Underline key points in the question: look for the word 'change', what is changing (life in the Soviet Union); and the time frame (the 1930s).
- Ensure that you focus on change. Begin each paragraph by stating the change and then fully develop each change you give.
- Aim to write about at least two, preferably three changes.
- Make links between one change and the next. Use link words or phrases, such as 'furthermore', 'moreover', 'however', 'in addition', 'as a result of', and 'this led to'.

The diagram on the right gives you further guidance on how to answer this type of question.

STEP 1 State the change.

Example: The first change was in the position of Stalin, who was able to remove his rivals and establish a dictatorship ruled by himself and the Communist Party.

STEP 2 Fully explain the change.

Example: Stalin was determined to remove any potential threats to his dictatorship by removing potential rivals and ensuring that, through terror, no one would dare threaten his position. The show trials enabled him to publicly discredit leading Bolsheviks such as Kamenev and Bukharin and finally remove the remaining Old Bolsheviks (in other words, those who knew the truth about his part in the events of 1917-24 and his relationship with Lenin). In 1935 many senior Communists were arrested, including 1108 out of 1966 delegates to the Seventeenth Congress.

STEP 3 Try to make links between each of the changes (paragraphs). Remember to use link words or phrases, such as 'furthermore', 'moreover', 'however', 'in addition', 'as a result of', and 'this led to'. This is an example of a possible link between the first change and the second.

Example: Moreover, the armed forces also presented a serious threat to his position as dictator, more especially Marshall Tukhachevsky, one of the heroes of the Civil War.

STEP 4 Go back to step 2 and have a go at completing the question by fully explaining the second change, linking it to a third one if you can.

Have a go yourself

9 Propaganda and censorship

> **Source A:** Extract from a speech by A. Avdienko, a writer, to the Congress of Soviets, February 1935
>
> *All thanks to thee, O great educator, Stalin. I love a young woman with a renewed love and shall perpetuate myself in my children – all thanks to thee, great educator, Stalin. I shall be eternally happy and joyous, all thanks to thee, O great educator, Stalin. Everything belongs to thee, chief of our great country. And when the woman I love presents me with a child the first word it shall say will be:* **Stalin**.

> **Task**
>
> What can you learn from Source A about what some people thought about Stalin?

When Stalin became leader of the Soviet Union, he was aware that in order to secure his position, he needed to control every aspect of daily life. Collectivisation and the Five-Year Plans (see Chapters 10 and 11) were crucial to his aims but he realised that he also needed the mass support of the people. To secure this support he ensured that all Soviet citizens – adults and children – became aware of his own personal greatness. It became impossible to avoid seeing and hearing glowing references to Stalin. These references took the form of naming such things as towns, cities and mountains after him. Moreover, it was impossible to escape seeing his face – all aspects of cultural life praised him and his achievements. For most Soviet citizens, Stalin became the 'Universal Genius'. His policies would create the New Soviet Man who would reject old Russia and embrace the only true socialist way – that is, the way of Stalin.

This chapter will answer the following questions:

- What was the cult of Stalin?
- Why was culture controlled by Stalin?
- How did Stalin control religion?
- What changes were made in education?
- What was the new constitution of 1936?

Examination skills

This chapter gives further guidance on question 2a from Unit 2. This question, which is worth eight marks, can be one of two types: either a change, or an 'explain how' question. This chapter looks at the 'explain how' question.

What was the cult of Stalin?

One of the key features of any **totalitarian state** is to glorify the leader and turn them into an almost god-like being. This 'cult of personality' was developed by Stalin, using the skills of propaganda he had developed as editor of *Pravda*.

Stalin's name and picture were everywhere. Streets and cities were named after him and poems and plays were written about him. Newspapers constantly carried stories of his wonderful achievements and they gave him nicknames such as 'Man of Steel', 'Shining Sun of Humanity' or *Vozhd* (the Boss). He created the image of himself as a caring leader whose genius had saved the Soviet Union from its enemies and made it the envy of the world. Huge parades in Red Square in Moscow, films, statues and paintings all showed how fortunate the Soviet people were to have such a great leader.

Artists, writers and film-makers were instructed to produce works in praise of Stalin and his achievements. Ordinary people were told that Stalin was the centre of all that was good and wise. He promised to reward those who were loyal to him with better housing and promotion at work. Party members, such as Avdienko in Source B, were forever praising his achievements.

Source A: Propaganda poster of Stalin from the 1930s

Source B: Extract from a speech by A. Avdienko, a writer, to the Seventh Congress of Soviets in February, 1935

Thank you Stalin. Thank you because I am joyful. Thank you because I am well. No matter how old I become, I shall never forget how we received Stalin two days ago. Centuries will pass, and the generations still to come will regard us as the happiest of mortals, as the most fortunate of men, because we lived in the century of centuries, because we were privileged to see Stalin, our inspired leader.

Tasks

1. *Explain why Stalin introduced the 'cult of personality'. (Remember how to answer this type of question? For further guidance, see page 74.)*

2. *What image does Source A give of Stalin? How does the artist create this image?*

3. *Why is Source B helpful in enabling you to understand the adoration of Stalin?*

Key Topic 3 The nature of Stalin's dictatorship, 1924–39

Changing history?

Stalin had to rewrite history to glorify his own part in the past, especially the Bolshevik **Revolution**, and remove that of 'enemies' such as Trotsky and other leading Bolsheviks. Photographs, such as the one on page 75, were doctored so that these people disappeared from Soviet history. In this way, images of Bukharin, Zinoviev and Kamenev were eventually removed from photographs.

At the same time, new photographs and histories were created, emphasising Stalin's role, especially his apparent close links with Lenin, who was still treated as a god in Soviet society. Stalin even encouraged the 'cult of Lenin' but with himself close at hand. Photographs were faked to show Stalin close to Lenin (see Source C).

Source C: A fake photograph. Stalin (right) has been added to this photograph of Lenin, originally taken in 1922

Source D: A patriotic painting showing Lenin directing the shelling of the Winter Palace during the 1917 revolution. The artist has placed Stalin in a prominent position among Lenin's aides

Tasks

4. Explain how Sources C and D help you understand why Stalin changed history.

5. You are a Soviet historian who has been asked to rewrite the Bolshevik Revolution of 1917 to greatly enhance the part played by Stalin.

   a) Look at pages 41–46 to see what actually happened.

   b) Now rewrite the events of October/November to show that Stalin played a key role.

Chapter 9 Propaganda and censorship

How was culture controlled by Stalin?

Stalin saw writers and artists as dangerous. All their work was carefully censored. It had to be submitted to committees before it was published, as described in Source A.

> **Source A:** From Victor Serge's *Memoirs of a Revolutionary*, 1945
>
> *Censorship, in many forms, mutilated or murdered books. Before sending a manuscript to the publisher, an author would assemble his friends, read his work to them and discuss together whether such-and-such pages would 'pass'. The head of the publishing group would then consult the Gavlit, or Literature Office, which censored manuscripts and proofs.*

This widespread propaganda campaign was directed particularly at children. Children were taught that Stalin was the 'Great Leader'. They learnt Stalin's version of history.

Writers, artists, film-makers and even composers had to support the government by following the policy of '**social realism**'. Music, art, poetry and plays had to be intelligible to the ordinary person and anything abstract was frowned upon. Great composers such as Shostakovich and Prokofiev were ordered to write only music that all could understand. This meant that many of the new artistic developments of the early twentieth century could not be reflected in Soviet culture.

The result was that artists' work had to deal with ordinary people, and had to show how communism was developing. Above all, it had to give simple, clear and optimistic messages. All aspects of culture would show the successes of communism and there had to be no doubt that the Soviet Union was a happy, fulfilling country for its citizens.

The Union of Soviet Writers was founded in 1934 to control the content of the work of authors. Any artists who deviated from the official Communist Party line were severely punished and many who fell foul of the Union were sent to the *gulag* labour camps in Siberia.

Source B: Photograph of a sculpture by Vera Mukhina, 1937. The title of the work is 'A worker and a woman collective farmer'

Tasks

1. What can you learn from Source A about censorship under Stalin?

2. In what ways does Source B help you understand social realist forms of art?

How did Stalin control religion?

There were three main religious groups that Stalin had to deal with – Russian Orthodox, Muslim and Jewish. Religious groups posed a threat to the 'cult of Stalin' as they owed their allegiance to a different god. Stalin continued and extended the Bolshevik attack on religion:

- Christian leaders were imprisoned
- More than 60,000 places of worship were closed down
- The 'League of the Godless' smashed churches and burned religious pictures
- Mosques and Muslim schools were closed and pilgrimages to Mecca were banned. Islamic law was banned and women were encouraged to unveil
- Jewish schools, libraries and synagogues were closed down. The study of Hebrew was banned.

However, despite these measures, it is thought that in the 1937 census, about 50 million Soviet citizens said they had religious beliefs. Some churches were permitted to remain open in the late 1930s – and by allowing this, Stalin could say that the idea of 'freedom of conscience' contained in the 1936 Constitution (see page 92) was being followed.

Source A: A poster against the Church published in 1932 entitled 'The Kingdom of the Church – A Kingdom in Chains'

Tasks

1. What message does Source A give about the Orthodox Church?

2. *Explain why Stalin controlled religion in the Soviet Union.* (Remember how to answer this type of question? For further guidance, see page 74.)

What changes were made in education?

What changes were made in education?

In 1932 a rigid programme of education was introduced. The Bolsheviks had introduced many new methods, which had not brought the progress they expected. Stalin returned to more traditional methods. Discipline was strict and examinations were brought back. There were even fees in some of the advanced secondary schools.

Children were taught that Stalin was the 'Great Leader'. They learnt Stalin's version of history. He even had a new book, 'A Short History of the USSR', written for school students, which showed him playing a more important role in the revolution. The teaching of communist **ideology** became compulsory in schools and, in addition, Stalin chose the subjects and information that children should learn.

Education changed to focus on the technical and scientific skills needed by Soviet workers who were involved in the Five-Year Plans (see page 106). Stalin did not wish to rely too long on foreign technicians. By 1939, 94 per cent of urban dwellers and 86 per cent of the rural population were able to read and write. Furthermore, the Soviet Union was producing a high number of engineers, teachers, doctors and scientists.

> **Source A:** Rule One of the Twenty Rules of Behaviour. Pupils had to learn these rules by heart
>
> It is the duty of each school child to acquire knowledge persistently so as to become an educated and cultured citizen and to be of the greatest possible service to his country.

> **Source B:** From the memoirs of Nadezhda Mandelstam, written in 1971. She was a poet whose husband, Osip, was purged and died in a prison camp
>
> Varia showed us her school textbooks where the portraits of the Communist Party leaders had thick pieces of paper pasted over them as one by one they fell into disgrace. The children had to do this on the instructions of their teacher.

> **Source C:** A Russian official describes educational progress in Russia by 1938
>
> During the twenty-one years of the existence of the Soviet Union this aspect of the country has undergone a radical change. A formerly backward and poverty-stricken country has now become an enlightened, cultured and strong socialist power. Half the population are studying in elementary, secondary and higher schools. Illiteracy has now been completely obliterated. In the school year of 1914–15 there were only 155,000 children between the ages of eight and eleven years in the schools of Georgia. Now there are 658,000 such school children.

Outside school, Stalin also wanted some control over the young. Children joined political youth groups, which trained them in socialism and communism. The youth groups were taught activities such as sports, camping and model-making, and there were different groups for different ages:

- 8 to 10-year-olds joined the Octobrists
- 10 to 16-year-olds joined the Young Pioneers
- 16 to 28-year-olds joined the Komsomol.

> **Source D:** The promise made by each member of the Young Pioneers
>
> *I, a Young Pioneer of the Soviet Union, in the presence of my comrades, solemnly promise to love my Soviet motherland passionately, and to live, learn and struggle as the great Lenin bade us and the Communist Party teaches us.*

Source E: A photograph of some Young Pioneers in Moscow in 1926

Tasks

1. What can you learn from Source A about what was expected of schoolchildren in the Soviet Union?

2. Study Source B. what was the purpose of forcing schoolchildren to paste over the photographs of disgraced Soviet leaders?

3. *Explain the effects on education of the changes introduced by Stalin.* (Remember how to answer this type of question? For further guidance, see page 60.)

4. Can you trust what this Soviet official has written in Source C? Explain your answer.

5. What image do Sources D and E give of the Young Pioneers?

What was the new constitution of 1936?

In 1936 Stalin introduced a new constitution. This was to convince Soviet citizens and the outside world that the USSR was a 'free' society. In fact, it merely served to confirm Stalin's dictatorship. The USSR was now composed of eleven socialist republics. The old Congress of the Soviets of the USSR became the **Supreme Soviet** or parliament of the USSR, with two chambers - the Soviet of the Union and the Soviet of Nationalities.

The Communist Party kept close control of both the central government and the government of each republic. Stalin held the posts of Prime Minister in the government, General Secretary of the Party and Chairman of the Party's Politburo. Stalin described the constitution as 'the most democratic in the world'. Its key features were:
- Secret ballots
- Elections to the Soviets every four years
- Candidates for elections had to be approved by the Communist Party
- Universal suffrage (voting rights) for all over the age of 18
- Guaranteed civil liberties such as: freedom of speech, press, assembly, religion and freedom from arbitrary arrest.

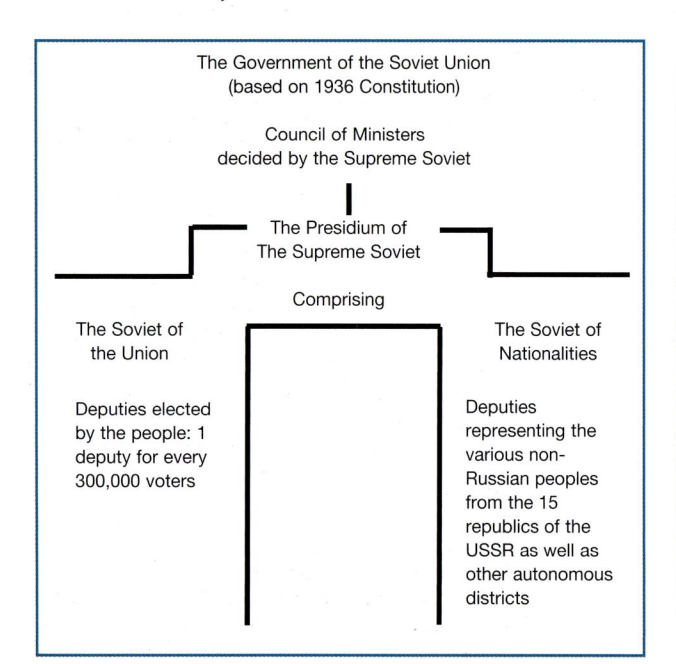

> **Source A:** Article 12 of the 1936 constitution
>
> *In the USSR work is a duty and a matter of honour for every able-bodied citizen in accordance with the principle 'He who does not work, neither shall he eat.' The principle applied in the USSR is that of socialism – 'From each according to his ability, to each according to his work.'*

However, the Constitution made it clear that the freedoms were to be exercised only with the approval of the Communist Party. Moreover, the Communist Party was the only party permitted to exist within the USSR. In elections, the Party candidate would be the only candidate and sometimes the results were announced before voting took place.

Despite the claims made by Stalin about the new constitution, real power lay with the Communist Party. There were no elections for bodies in the Communist Party – members were chosen. The two most important parts were the Politburo and the Central Committees but these did not always meet on a regular basis and Stalin made all decisions with his group of close advisers.

The Government of the Soviet Union (based on 1936 Constitution)

Council of Ministers decided by the Supreme Soviet

The Presidium of The Supreme Soviet

Comprising

- **The Soviet of the Union** — Deputies elected by the people: 1 deputy for every 300,000 voters
- **The Soviet of Nationalities** — Deputies representing the various non-Russian peoples from the 15 republics of the USSR as well as other autonomous districts

Tasks

1. Explain why Stalin introduced the constitution in 1936. (Remember how to answer this type of question? For further guidance, see page 74.)

2. Was the constitution democratic? Complete the table below.

Democratic	Undemocratic

3. Study Source A. Explain what is meant by the phrase 'From each according to his ability, to each according to his work.'

Examination practice

This section provides guidance on how to answer question 2a from Unit 2, which is worth eight marks. This is the 'explain how' question and is similar to the 'change' question explained on page 84.

Question 1 – 'explain how'
Explain how Stalin developed the cult of personality in the 1930s. (8 marks)

How to answer
- Underline key points in the question: look for the key theme (developing the cult of personality), the command word (explain) and the time frame (1930s).
- Ensure that you focus on specific points. Begin each paragraph by stating the point and then fully develop each point you mention.
- Aim to write about at least two points, and preferably three.
- Make links between one point and the next. Use link words or phrases, such as 'furthermore', 'moreover', 'however', 'in addition', 'as a result of', and 'this led to'.

The diagram on the right gives you further guidance on how to answer this type of question.

STEP 1 State the point.

Example: When Stalin became leader he needed to gain the support of the Russian people.

STEP 2 Fully explain the point.

Example: He gained this support by turning himself into a god-like figure that the population eventually worshipped. He made sure that his name was mentioned in the same breath as Lenin and, furthermore, paintings and photographs always showed him close to the leader of the Revolution. In fact, Stalin was careful to show that his own position in the Revolution was greater than it had been.

STEP 3 Try to make links between each of the points (paragraphs). Remember to use link words or phrases, such as 'furthermore', 'moreover', 'however', 'in addition', 'as a result of', and 'this led to'. This is an example of a possible link between the first point and the second.

Example: In addition, Stalin insisted that he became known as the Universal Genius or the 'Boss' – the man who was saving the Soviet Union and above all was making it the most powerful nation in the world.

STEP 4 Fully explain the point.

Example: Stalin claimed that only his policies would save the Soviet Union and he put out this message by making sure that all successes were recorded for all to see. His face was seen everywhere in posters, newspapers wrote of his genius, he was seen as the father not only of the country but all the young children. He truly wanted to be seen as the saviour.

STEP 5 Now, finish this answer by writing about a third point. This could be about naming towns, cities, rivers and streets after himself.

Have a go yourself

Question 2 – 'explain how'
Explain how Stalin used culture to control the citizens of the Soviet Union in the 1930s. (8 marks)

Now have a go yourself
Try answering question 2 using the steps shown for question 1. Remember to:
- write about at least two points
- make links between each point.

Key Topic 4: Economic and social changes, 1928–39

> **Source A:** From *Stalin and Khrushchev* by M. Lynch, 2001
>
> *What Stalin's massive restructuring of agriculture did was to put an end to uncertainty and argument. From 1928 onwards, with the introduction of **collectivisation** and **industrialisation**, there were no doubts concerning the Soviet Union's economic strategies. The Soviet state would take over the running of the nation's economy. This momentous decision is often referred to by historians as 'the second **revolution**'.*

> **Task**
>
> *What can you learn from Source A about Stalin and the economy of the Soviet Union? (Remember how to answer this type of question? For further guidance, see page 24.)*

When Stalin became leader of the Soviet Union in 1928, he was aware that he faced many huge tasks. You have already seen in the previous key topic how he rose to power and secured his position. This key topic looks at how Stalin modernised agriculture and industry so that the Soviet Union could compete with the industrialised world. Moreover, by modernising the Soviet Union, Stalin recognised that he would be able to secure even greater control over the Soviet people. Thus his **Five-Year Plans** and collectivisation were a double-edged sword. The impact of his modernisation policies can be seen in Chapter 12.

Each chapter explains a key issue and examines important lines of enquiry as outlined below:

Chapter 10 Collectivisation (pages 95–104)

- Why did Stalin decide to modernise Soviet agriculture?
- Why did Stalin decide on collectivisation?
- How were collective farms organised?
- What were the effects of collectivisation?
- What opposition was there to collectivisation?

Chapter 11 Industrialisation (pages 105–114)

- What were the Five-Year Plans?
- What results did the Five-Year Plans have?
- What changes took place in working and living conditions?

Chapter 12 Life in the Soviet Union (pages 115–121)

- What were the experiences of different social groups?
- Did the position of women change?
- Why were ethnic groups persecuted?
- Did living conditions worsen under Stalin?

10 Collectivisation

Source A: Wheat threshing on a collective farm in the 1930s

Task

What can you learn from Source A about **collective farms** in the Soviet Union in 1933?

Stalin was determined to modernise the Soviet economy. He introduced a series of Five-Year Plans that transformed industry and a policy of collectivisation, which brought major changes to agriculture. In some respects farming had not changed for hundreds of years and, before collectivisation, many farms still followed the medieval system of farming strips of land using horse-drawn wooden ploughs.

This chapter answers the following questions:
- Why did Stalin decide to modernise Soviet agriculture?
- Why did Stalin decide on collectivisation?
- How were collective farms organised?
- What were the effects of collectivisation?
- What opposition was there to collectivisation?

Examination skills
In this chapter you will be given the opportunity to practise some of the question types from Unit 2.

Why did Stalin decide to modernise Soviet agriculture?

> **Source A:** From a speech by Stalin in February 1931. He was talking about the backwardness of the Soviet Union
>
> *We must create in our country an industry which would be capable of re-equipping and organising the whole of our industry but also our transport and agriculture. The history of Russia shows that because of her backwardness she was constantly defeated. Those that fall behind get beaten. No, we refuse to be beaten. We are 50 and 100 years behind the advanced countries. We must make good this distance in ten years. Either we do it, or we shall be crushed.*

Stalin wanted to transform the USSR from a backward agricultural country to a modern industrial one. His rationale was based on a combination of economic and political factors that were linked by a fear of foreign invasion. Furthermore, he believed that if the Soviet Union was to compete with the industrialised nations of the world, then the only way to do this was by state intervention. He was also aware that any intervention by the state in agriculture and industry would lead to greater control over the people of the Soviet Union.

Stalin made it clear that workers would have to accept personal sacrifices in pursuit of these targets. He also put forward reasons why modernisation had to take place.

Fear of invasion

The help given by Britain, France and the USA to the Whites during the civil war of 1918–21 (see pages 56–57) seemed to confirm Stalin's fears of an attack from the West. Industrialisation was essential if the Soviet Union was to be sure of victory in any future war. It would enable him to build up and control the armed forces. There were several war scares in the USSR in the late 1920s and there was a growing feeling of **diplomatic isolation** among many leading politicians. The modernisation of industry and agriculture would strengthen the country and, they hoped, deter any would-be opponent.

Disappointing output

Soviet industrial production remained disappointingly low. Stalin felt that central direction and control would enable him to direct the economy and ensure a rapid expansion in heavy industry in order to outstrip the developed nations.

Communist principles

Stalin also had political reasons to modernise Soviet agriculture and industry. By creating and sharing wealth among the Soviet people he hoped to create a strong state based on communist principles, where the state controlled economic activity.

Leadership

Furthermore, industrialisation would consolidate Stalin's position as leader and give him total control of these areas. The **right-wing** members of the Communist Party's *Politburo*, Bukharin, Tomsky and Rykov, were in favour of keeping the **New Economic Policy**. The launching of the Five-Year Plans would enable Stalin to discredit and remove these leading figures and, by 1929, he felt more secure in his position as leader of the Party.

> **Task**
>
> Create a concept map of the reasons behind Stalin's decision to modernise agriculture. Explain which you think is the most important.

Why did Stalin decide on collectivisation?

What was collectivisation?

Collectivisation meant that peasants had to give up their small plots of land and animals and pool them with those of other families in order to make a farm large enough to use machinery and modern farming methods. The idea was to create a surplus of food through employing these methods.

> **Source A:** From a speech about problems in agriculture by Stalin to the Communist Party Congress in 1927
>
> *What is the way out? The way out is to turn the small and scattered peasant farms into large united farms based on cultivation of the land in common … on the basis of a new higher technique. The way out is to unite the small and very small peasant farms gradually but surely, not by pressure but by example and persuasion into large farms based on common co-operative collective cultivation of the land.*

> **Source B:** A Communist Party official speaking to peasants about collectivisation, 1930
>
> *Tell me. You wretched people, what hope is there for you if you remain on individual pieces of land? From year to year you divide and sub-divide your strips of land. You cannot even use machinery on your land because no machine could stand the rough ridges that the strip system creates. Don't you see that there is nothing ahead of you but ruin and starvation?*

As we have seen, a mixture of economic and political motives lay behind Stalin's decision to change Soviet agriculture. Some of these are outlined in more detail below and on page 98.

The grain crisis of 1927

Before collectivisation, Soviet peasants used old-fashioned, inefficient farming methods. Agriculture was still based on small peasant plots with little use of machinery. Even under the New Economic Policy (see pages 65–66), farmers were not producing enough food for the workers in the cities. After 1926, the amount of surplus grain given to the government by the peasants had been falling. The peasants had become wary of growing too much food, knowing it would be seized by the state at a low price. There was said to be a 'grain crisis' in 1927 and Stalin was keen to ensure adequate supplies for workers in the cities.

Industrialisation

Industrialisation was to be supported by the food surpluses that collectivisation was supposed to create. Stalin knew that the West would not lend the Soviet Union money, nor could he expect any investment from foreign countries. The agricultural surpluses would be sold abroad and would therefore finance the initial stages of the Five-Year Plans. (The Five-Year Plans were Stalin's strategy for changing the Soviet Union to a highly industrialised country that could compete with the major powers of the world. These plans are examined in more detail in Chapter 11, see pages 105–114.)

> **Task**
>
> 1. What can you learn from Sources A and B about collectivisation?

The needs of industrialisation

If the Five-Year Plans were to be successful, agriculture had to be modernised. Mechanisation was the key, because it would release large numbers of peasants to work in the towns and cities. Fewer peasants, therefore, would have to produce more food, as even greater numbers of workers would have to be fed. Stalin had created a problem for himself. He needed workers to create machinery for industry and agriculture but, to do this, peasants would have to move into towns. Yet this would reduce the number of workers on the land and he needed agricultural production to increase in order to sell food abroad to bring in foreign currency to allow him to invest in materials for his factories. It was insoluble – unless some sections were to starve.

Source C: Soviet grain exports 1929–32 in millions of tonnes

1929	1930	1931	1932
0.18	4.76	5.06	1.73

Source D: Extracts from speeches made about collectivisation by Stalin in 1928 and 1929

*Look at the kulak farms: their barns and sheds are crammed with grain. They are waiting for prices to rise. So long as there are kulaks there will be sabotage of our grain needs. The effect will be that our towns and industrial centres, as well as the **Red Army**, will be threatened with hunger. We cannot allow that. We must break the resistance of this class and deprive it of its existence.*

Source E: From a speech by Stalin to the Communist Party of the Soviet Union in 1929. Here he was threatening the *kulaks*

We must eliminate the kulaks as a class. We must smash the kulaks ... we must strike at the kulaks so hard as to prevent them from rising to their feet again. We must annihilate them as a social class.

Destroy the *kulaks*

Stalin also had political motives. He disliked the richer peasants – the *kulaks* – who, in the eyes of the communists, hoarded food for their own consumption, rather than providing it for industrial workers in the towns. This is clearly shown in Sources D and E.

There was increasing pressure on the government to remove this capitalist class. However, the majority of the peasants were not *kulaks* and any changes to the farming system – especially collectivisation – would be met by opposition from a large number of them. Most peasants were by nature conservative in

Source F: Peasants protesting against the *kulaks*

outlook, and they had already shown in the civil war and the 1920s that they were not completely convinced by the theories of the Bolsheviks.

Communist ideals

Collectivisation fitted in with communist ideas of common ownership. In 1925, as a result of the New Economic Policy (see pages 66–67), less than one per cent of the land was collectivised. Moreover, the policy would also enable Stalin to strengthen his dictatorship. He would be able to discredit the Right, led by Bukharin, who supported the New Economic Policy and opposed collectivisation.

Control of the countryside

As well as wanting to modernise the Soviet Union, Stalin also sought to control the people – this time the peasants – through collectivisation. This would give Stalin control over the countryside and the peasantry, something that Lenin had failed to achieve. Stalin did not trust the peasants. He saw them as natural enemies of communism and he was aware of how close they had come to destroying Lenin during the time of War Communism (see pages 62–63). He believed that by taking away the peasants' independence, gained as a result of their ownership of the land, he could remove any threat from them once and for all.

Source G: Soviet cartoon of a peasant working on his own plot of land rather than in the collective

Tasks

2. Look at all Stalin's motives for collectivisation on pages 97–99 and put them in order of importance, beginning with the one you think is the most important. Give a brief explanation for each choice you make. If you work in small groups, you can compare lists and see if there is any agreement.

3. How effective do you think Source G would be in turning the Soviet people against the kulaks? Give reasons for your answer.

4. Study Sources D, E and G. Explain why Stalin was keen to focus on the kulaks *as enemies of the state*.

5. Describe the key features of collectivisation. (Remember how to answer this type of question? For further guidance, see page 39.)

How were the collective farms organised?

Collectivisation was supposed to be undertaken on a voluntary basis, but within a year it was being imposed on the peasants. Anyone who opposed the process was labelled as a *kulak* and an enemy of the state and deported to Siberia and the Urals.

Kolkhoz

The Russian word for a collective farm is *kolkhoz* and it replaced the *mir* or village commune.

Local Communist Party officials went into villages and explained how the collective farm or *kolkhoz* would be organised. The most important figure in the *kolkhoz* was the chairman, who was a Communist Party member, usually from the nearest town. Once established, the *kolkhoz* would then claim ownership of animals, grain supplies and buildings in the village.

By 1940, there were about 240,000 *kolkhoz*. They were normally made up of 80 or so peasant families who farmed around 500 hectares of land. The families had to provide a fixed amount of food for the state at very low prices and peasants received a small wage. The peasants could keep any surplus. Members of the *kolkhoz* also had their own private plots of land.

The state provided each collective farm with machinery, especially a tractor, other tools and seeds. In addition, Machine Tractor Stations (MTS) were set up. There was normally one of these for every 40 collective farms. Tractors and drivers from the MTS moved between the collectives to carry out the ploughing. By 1933, there were some 2900 MTS, which controlled more than 120,000 tractors. Members of the secret police were employed in some of the first MTS. This was another means by which Stalin was able to gain political control over the peasants.

Source A: A propaganda photograph of 1931 showing Russian peasants enthusiastically queuing up to join a collective. The photograph was used across the Soviet Union and was entitled 'We would like to work together'

Source B: A mid-twentieth century Soviet painting of life in a *kolkhoz*

Sovkhoz

There was also a type of farm called a *sovkhoz*, which was usually created from the old, large estates. In the *sovkhoz*, all land was owned by the state and all produce was taken by the state. The *sovkhoz* was usually about 3600 hectares and, unlike the *kolkhoz*, had its own tractors. The peasants worked as paid labourers and were referred to as workers. One historian has called the *sovkhoz* 'a factory without a roof'.

> ### Tasks
>
> **1.** *Explain the effects of collectivisation on Soviet agriculture. (Remember how to answer this type of question? For further guidance, see page 60.)*
>
> **2.** *Describe the key features of a kolkhoz. (Remember how to answer this type of question? For further guidance, see page 39.)*
>
> **3.** Study Sources A and B. In what ways are these sources helpful to you in understanding collectivisation?

What were the effects of collectivisation?

1 Human cost
The human cost of collectivisation was enormous. There was a serious famine from 1932 to 1933, which caused the death of somewhere between six and ten million peasants.

Source A: Photograph of victims of the famine during the first phase of collectivisation, circa 1931

2 Benefits
The aim of producing enough food to feed the towns and the Red Army was achieved. Life on the collective farms was not all bad. For example, there were schools and hospitals on some collectives for the workers. The MTS (see page 100) were quite successful and the mechanisation of farming did speed up in the years after 1935. By 1936, more than 90 per cent of land had been collectivised and tractors were introduced on a large scale.

Effects of collectivisation

3 Fall in production
Economically, collectivisation had mixed results. Peasant opposition led to a serious decline in grain production, from 73.3 million tonnes in 1928 to 67.6 million in 1934. The impact on the countryside was worsened by the government policy of seizing grain. The rural population starved in order to provide for the needs of industry, and peasants moved to the towns in search of food. Such movement was stopped when the government introduced passports simply for moving around the country. The peasants thus became tied to the collectives and were little better off than the **serfs** of tsarist Russia.

Source B: The figures below are Western estimates based on Soviet statistics

Consumption of foodstuffs (in kilos per head)

	Bread	Potatoes	Meat	Lard/Butter
1928	250.4	141.11	24.8	1.35
1932	214.6	125.0	11.2	0.7

Comparative numbers of livestock (in millions) and grain production (in million tonnes), 1929–35

	1929	1930	1931	1932	1933	1934	1935
Grain	71.7	83.5	69.5	69.6	68.4	67.6	75.0
Cattle	67.1	52.5	47.9	40.7	38.4	42.4	49.3
Pigs	20.4	13.6	14.4	11.6	12.1	17.4	22.6
Sheep/goats	147.0	108.8	77.7	52.1	50.2	51.9	61.1

4 Inefficient farming

Farming remained inefficient, with Soviet farmers producing less per head than farmers in the USA or Western Europe. Until the mid-1930s, there was not enough food grown for the whole Soviet population and some had to be bought from abroad. The worst years were 1932–33 when a national famine occurred. In the Ukraine and the northern Caucasus about five million people died. It was not until 1940 that figures for grain production matched those of 1914. Historians have found little evidence that collectivisation provided surplus food to sell abroad and the strategy therefore failed to provide adequate foreign capital for Stalin's investment programme.

5 Greater control

Collectivisation was also a success for Stalin and the communists. They had finally secured control of the countryside. The peasants never again openly rebelled against communist rule. Stalin had also ensured that he had a secure supply of food for the towns and workers for the factories.

> **Source C:** From a report by a government official in 1933. He was writing about collectivisation
>
> It took a famine to show the peasants who was master.

Tasks

1. What can you learn from Source A about the effects of collectivisation?

2. Look at the effects of collectivisation.

a) Organise the effects into successes and failures and set out your answer as a two-column table as below.

Successes	Failures

b) Overall, do you think the successes outweigh the failures?

3. Study Source B.

a) What can you learn from the source about the impact of collectivisation on food production?

b) Why do think that the provenance of the source says 'Western estimates based on Soviet statistics'?

4. What does Source C mean? Explain your answer.

5. *Was his desire to gain control of the kulaks the main reason for Stalin introducing collectivisation after 1928? Explain your answer.*

You may use the following information to help you with your answer.

- *Control of the kulaks*
- *Famine*
- *Secure his position*
- *Help the Soviet Union to industrialise*

(For guidance on answering this type of question, see pages 113–114.)

What opposition was there to collectivisation?

There was fierce opposition to collectivisation, especially in the agricultural areas of the Ukraine and Caucasus. Many peasants set fire to their farms and slaughtered their animals, rather than hand them over to the state. The scale of the slaughter was staggering – from a total of 60 million cows, 30 million were killed, and 16 million horses died out of a total of 34 million. This is clearly explained in Source A.

> **Source A:** From *Virgin Soil Upturned*, a novel by M. Sholokov, 1934. Sholokov lived in the Soviet Union during the period of collectivisation
>
> *Both those who had joined the kolkhoz and individual farmers killed their stock. Bulls, sheep, pigs and even cows were slaughtered. The dogs began to drag entrails around the village; cellars and barns were full of meat. Young and old suffered from stomach ache. At dinner times tables groaned under boiled and roasted meat.*

De-kulakisation

Stalin retaliated by sending in de-kulakisation squads – Party members from the towns and the **OGPU** – to round up opponents of his policy as explained in Source B. It is impossible to find an accurate figure, but possibly as many as ten million people were deported in the war against the *kulaks*.

The extent of opposition forced Stalin to slow down the process of collectivisation in 1930. Indeed, he blamed over-keen Party officials for the problems in carrying out his policy and, during the spring and summer of that year, there was some reversal of the process. He also made some concessions, including allowing members of the collectives to have some animals and a small garden plot for their own use. However, in late 1930, collectivisation began again. By 1932, 62 per cent of peasant households had been collectivised, and five years later the number had increased to 93 per cent.

> **Source B:** From Victor Kravchenko's book *I Chose Freedom*. He witnessed collectivisation and the attack on the *kulaks* in one village. Kravchenko was a high-ranking Soviet official in the 1930s who eventually sought political asylum in the USA
>
> *A number of women were weeping hysterically and calling the names of their fathers and husbands. In the background, guarded by the OGPU and soldiers with drawn revolvers, stood about twenty peasants, young and old, with bundles on their backs. A few were weeping. The others stood there sad and helpless. So this was 'liquidation of the kulaks as a class'. A lot of simple peasants being torn from their native soil, stripped of all their worldly goods and shipped to some distant labour camps.*

Tasks

1. What were the immediate effects of collectivisation?

2. What does Source B show you about the *kulaks* and collectivisation?

3. *Explain why the kulaks were so opposed to collectivisation.* (Remember how to answer this type of question? For further guidance, see page 74.)

11 Industrialisation

Task

Look at Source A. Why do you think workers were encouraged to study this table?

Source A: A photograph of workers looking at a league table, which shows the production levels for other factories

Stalin was determined to modernise Soviet industry as quickly as possible. For this reason he introduced a series of targets for industry known as the Five-Year Plans. These brought about rapid growth, especially of heavy industry, and provided employment opportunities for women. However, this was achieved at a cost – often poor working and living conditions for workers and the use of slave labour from the *gulags*.

This chapter answers the following questions:

- What were the Five-Year Plans?
- What results did the Five-Year Plans have?
- What changes took place in working and living conditions?

Examination skills

This chapter gives guidance on answering question 3 from Unit 2. This question, which is worth sixteen marks, is a scaffolding question.

What were the Five-Year Plans?

Stalin's motives for industrialisation

In the years after 1928 Stalin introduced a series of Five-Year Plans. These plans set production targets for Soviet industry. Workers in each industry were told exactly how much they must produce. Stalin believed that the Five-Year Plans were the only way to transform the Soviet Union into an industrial power in a short space of time. He was convinced that the Soviet Union would be invaded by the surrounding capitalist countries. Only a strong industrial economy could produce the wealth and modern weapons that the Soviet Union needed if it was to survive such an attack.

In addition Stalin strongly opposed the New Economic Policy (NEP) because it allowed private enterprise and went against the ideals of communism. He was determined to restore central or state direction of industry, which would in turn give him full control of Soviet industry.

In 1928, the NEP was abandoned and the first Five-Year Plan was launched. This was to be directed by **Gosplan** (the State Planning Authority), which set the targets for certain key industries and ensured that these industries were given priority in the allocation of manpower and raw materials.

The targets set were often very unrealistic and Stalin's response to those who said that the pace of industrialisation was too fast was '. . .those who lag behind are beaten'.

The First Five-Year Plan, 1928–32

The first Five-Year Plan (1928–32) concentrated on heavy industry, such as coal, steel and iron. The 'new' industries, such as electricity, motor vehicles, chemicals and rubber, were also targeted but consumer industries, such as textiles and household goods, were neglected.

Stalin was encouraged by the apparent success of the plan and he revised the targets twice – the table in Source B shows the original and revised targets alongside the actual figures.

Source A: A 1930 photograph of the first tractor produced at the Stalingrad Tractor Works

Source B: Table showing industrial output during the first Five-Year Plan

Production (in million tonnes)	1927-28 Original targets	1932-33 'optimal' (highest expected)	1932 revised targets	1932 actual output
Coal	35.0	75.0	95–105	64.0
Oil	11.7	21.7	40–55	21.4
Iron Ore	6.7	20.2	24–32	12.1
Pig Iron	3.2	10.0	15–16	6.2

Tasks

1. Study Source A. This was used as a propaganda photo. Devise a suitable caption for this photo.

2. What can you learn from Source B about the first Five-Year Plan? (Remember how to answer this type of question? For further guidance, see page 24.)

Thousands of Soviet citizens, especially young people, willingly went to work in the new towns and factories, because they genuinely believed that they were creating a new society.

The Second Five-Year Plan, 1933–37

The Second Five-Year Plan did, at first, set targets for the increased production of consumer goods. Some of the mistakes of the first plan, such as setting targets that were too high, were avoided. As fears of invasion from the West increased, especially from Nazi Germany, heavy industry again became the priority. During the second plan, the production of **armaments** trebled.

Living standards did not increase and strikes were not permitted.

The Third Five-Year Plan, 1938–41

This was launched in 1938, but was abandoned when Germany invaded the Soviet Union in June 1941. It concentrated on the production of household goods and luxury items, such as bicycles and radios.

The figures in Source C are drawn from the work of the economic historian E. Zaleki, whose findings are based on careful analysis of Soviet and Western sources. They give an overview of industrial production during the Five-Year Plans.

Source C: Table showing industrial output during the Five-Year Plans

Production (in million tonnes)	1927	1930	1932	1935	1937	1940
Coal	35	60	64	100	128	150
Steel	3	5	6	13	18	18
Oil	12	17	21	24	26	26
Electricity	18	22	20	45	80	90

Source D: From a history of the USSR written by a Soviet historian in 1981

Whilst the economies of the capitalist states were sinking ever deeper into recession, the Soviet economy was booming. The second sections of the Magnitogorsk and Kuznetsk iron and steel complexes were completed ahead of schedule. At the start of the Five-Year Plan a major victory was scored on the industrialisation front when the Urals heavy engineering plants went into operation. Good progress was made in constructing new railways and motorways. During the second Five-Year Plan period, industrial output went up by 120 per cent.

Tasks

1. Describe the key features of the Five-Year Plans. *(Remember how to answer this type of question? For further guidance, see page 39.)*

2. What can you learn from Source D about the Five-Year Plans? *(Remember how to answer this type of question? For further guidance, see page 24.)*

3. Write a newspaper article about the Five-Year Plans, with the headline 'Stalin introduces revolutionary plans to modernise the Soviet Union'.

Chapter 11 Industrialisation

What results did the Five-Year Plans have?

Advances in industry

Although the plans' targets were not all met, all Soviet industries made remarkable advances and, by 1940, the USSR was the world's second-largest industrial power behind the USA. The second Five-Year Plan made greater use of technical expertise, with spectacular growth in the coal and chemical industries. However, oil production remained disappointing.

Stakhanovites

The miner Alexei Stakhanov became a hero of the Soviet Union when, on the night of 30–31 August 1935, it was claimed that he shifted 102 tonnes of coal, which was almost fifteen times the normal amount for a single shift. It was, however, a set-up. He had two helpers who removed the coal while he worked at the coalface with his pick. In the workplace, employees were urged to work harder through encouragement and the example of people such as Alexei Stakhanov (see photo below). Other workers were encouraged to follow Stakhanov's example and they formed '**shock brigades**' in attempts to copy their worker hero.

The **Stakhanovites**, as they were known, were rewarded with medals (the 'Order of Lenin' or 'Hero of the Soviet Union'), new houses, free holidays and other benefits. However, the campaign was quietly dropped in the late 1930s after a number of Stakhanovites were beaten up and killed by their fellow workers.

Tasks

1. What was meant by the term 'Stakhanovite movement'?

2. Why do you think Stalin considered the Stakhanovites to be so important?

3. *What can you learn from Source A about the location of industry during the Five-Year Plans?* (Remember how to answer this type of question? For further guidance, see page 24.)

4. *Study Source B. Why would this be used for propaganda purposes?*

5. *Explain the effects of the Five-Year Plans on Soviet industry.* (Remember how to answer this type of question? For further guidance, see page 60.)

Alexei Stakhanov explaining his working methods to fellow miners.

Key topic 4 Economic and social changes, 1929–38

Source A: Location of different types of industry during the Five-Year Plans

Changes in location and organisation of industry

As can be seen from Source A, much industry was located in the remoter areas of the USSR, east of the Ural Mountains, where industry would be safe against attack from the West. Huge towns and industrial centres were built from scratch deep inside the USSR. For example, Magnitogorsk concentrated on iron and steel. Little had existed there before the Five-Year Plan and workers were either encouraged or forced to to move to the site. In the space of three years, 1929–32, Magnitogorsk grew from 25 to 250,000 people.

In the years 1929–39, the population of the USSR's cities rose by 29 million. Vast construction projects were undertaken, such as the Dnieper Dam hydroelectric power station, the Belomor Canal, the Moscow underground and the Moscow-Volga canal.

Source B: Komsomol volunteers at a construction site at the new city of Komsomolsk, Siberia in the 1930s

A skilled workforce

In 1929 Soviet workers lacked many of the skills needed to carry out industrialisation. The workforce was essentially illiterate, unskilled and undisciplined. The main problems facing managers in factories were drunkenness and absenteeism – many workers returned to their villages after they had failed to come to terms with the discipline of factory life.

Between 1929 and 1937, investment in education and training schemes created a skilled workforce. A new **elite** emerged – teachers, scientists, engineers, factory managers and skilled workers, who were paid far higher wages than ordinary workers.

Like many officials, they also received extra benefits, such as better housing or the right to buy scarce foods. They enjoyed a higher standard of living, which went against communist principles, but Stalin realised that incentives had to be used in order to attract the right calibre of people.

Opportunities for women

Women were encouraged to work to help achieve the Five-Year Plans. Facilities such as crèches were provided to help them continue working after childbirth. There were some improvements in education and health for the workers and their families. All workers' children received free primary education and free healthcare schemes were extended to cover most of the workforce.

> **Source C:** A female machinist in a tractor factory in Stalingrad in the 1930s

> **Source D:** Soviet girls learning to read in a state-run literacy class in the 1930s

Over-ambitious targets

The targets of the Five-Year Plans were frequently too ambitious and set at unrealistic levels. As a result, some were not achieved. Officials at every level often gave false or exaggerated production figures in order to satisfy the demands of *Gosplan*. The production of textiles actually declined during the first Five-Year Plan and the housing industry was virtually ignored. Above all, there was a serious shortage of consumer goods.

Quality remained an over-riding problem in each of the plans. Many of the workers were peasants, with little experience of working with machines; for example, half the tractors produced for the collective farms soon broke down. Industry grew so rapidly that the shortage of skilled workers became a real problem, so much so that the first Five-Year Plan produced only 50,000 tractors, when the target was 170,000.

> ### Tasks
>
> 6. Why do you think that Stalin focused on eradicating illiteracy in the 1930s?
>
> 7. Can you suggest any disadvantages for Stalin if he had a literate workforce?
>
> 8. Study Sources C and D. Why do you think that many of the propaganda photographs about industrial change featured women?

What changes took place in working and living conditions?

Working and living conditions

Economic progress was often achieved at the expense of harsh living and working conditions. Some of the biggest tasks in the Five-Year Plans were carried out in appalling conditions by forced labour – prisoners in *gulags*. Many of these workers were peasants who had opposed collectivisation (see pages 95–97) and they built, among other projects, the Belomor Canal and the Moscow Metro. These conditions are described by an eyewitness in Source B.

Peasants were also pressed into working in the factories. They were not used to the harsh industrial regime and experienced terrible conditions, similar to the workers before the Revolution. Millions died as a result of Stalin's policies; and yet there were people who defended the vision Stalin put forward and believed that his policies meant a strong Soviet Union.

It proved impossible to build enough new houses for the millions of peasants who flooded into the cities or worked in the new industrial centres. Most families had to live in overcrowded and run-down buildings, such as those described in Source A.

Workers were poorly paid. The value of their wages fell by 50 per cent, meaning that something they could buy in 1928 cost them twice as much in 1933. There was a great shortage of everyday goods, and there were few workmen to carry out domestic repairs. Crime, alcoholism and juvenile delinquency increased.

Fines were imposed for lateness and bad workmanship, and workers who were absent for more than a day were sacked. Failures were always blamed on **saboteurs** rather than on the system. The secret police encouraged workers to inform on one another. Anyone blamed for obstructing work could be sent to a labour camp or shot. In 1928, 55 engineers working in the Shakhty coalmines in the Donbass were accused of sabotaging equipment and organising accidents and were put on trial. Despite their innocence, five were shot.

> **Source A:** A description of a Moscow apartment by Freda Utley, from her memoirs *Lost Illusion*, 1949. Utley was an American Marxist who lived in the Soviet Union during the 1930s
>
> *Badly built, with doors and windows of unseasoned wood, which could not be shut properly. Unpapered and thinly whitewashed walls, these two rooms were home. By American and British standards, we were living in a squalid tenement house. But by Soviet Russian standards we were housed almost as Communist aristocrats. We not only had two rooms to live in. We had the luxury of gas for cooking. Best of all we had a bathroom with a lavatory, which we had to share with only one other family.*

> **Source B:** An eyewitness account of conditions during the building of the Belomor Canal in the 1930s
>
> *At the end of the day there were corpses left on the worksite. Two were frozen back to back leaning against each other. At night sledges went out and collected them. In the summer, bones remained from corpses which had not been removed in time.*

Source C: Photograph showing working conditions on the Belomor Canal

Source D: A photograph showing working conditions in Magnitorgorsk in 1930

Source E: Khrushchev, in a speech made in 1956, after Stalin's death, about the effects of industrialisation. He was talking about how people just 'disappeared' in the 1930s

Both these managers perished in 1937. They disappeared off the face of the earth without leaving so much as a trace. Nobody could tell what happened to them. I don't know how many factory managers and engineers perished in this way. It was easy to get rid of someone you didn't like. All you had to do was submit a report denouncing him as an enemy of the people. The local party organisation would glance at your report and have the man taken care of.

Tasks

1. Study Sources A, B, C and D on pages 111–112. Do they suggest that industrialisation was a success or failure? Give reasons for your answer.

2. What does Source E suggest about the effects of industrialisation?

3. a) Make your own balance sheet showing the successes and failures of industrialisation. Set it out as a two-column table as in the example below.

Successes	Failures

b) Overall, do you think the successes outweigh the failures? Give reasons for your answer.

4. If living and working conditions were harsh, why were there so few strikes or demonstrations against them? (Look back to pages 108–109 to help you with this answer.)

Key topic 4 Economic and social changes, 1929–38

Examination practice

This section provides guidance on how to answer question 3 from Unit 2, which is worth sixteen marks – the most for any question. This is the scaffolding question because you are given four points (a 'scaffold') around which to build your essay answer.

Question – scaffolding

Was the employment of women the main effect of the Five-Year Plans?

> You may use the following information to help you with your answer.
> - The employment of women
> - Living and working conditions
> - Advances in industry
> - Changes in location of industry

(16 marks)

How to answer

- Ensure you do not simply describe the four parts of the scaffolding.
- Focus on the key words in the question, such as key dates, events and the main theme. This question is about the effects of the Five-Year Plans.
- Make use of at least three points from the scaffolding or develop at least three points of your own. The examiner will have assisted you by placing the points in chronological or topical order.
- You can make use of the scaffolding or add one or more points of your own not mentioned in the scaffolding – a skilled workforce, for example. Make it clear to the examiner that you are doing this.
- Remember to make a judgement about the importance of each factor and then an overall judgement at the end.
- Write an introduction that identifies the key areas you are going to explain in your answer.
- Write a conclusion that gives your overall judgement on the question. Remember, you need to make a decision on the relative importance of the points. You could decide that they were all equally important or two were more important. Give a reason for your judgement.

The sample on page 114 shows the steps you should take to write a good answer to a scaffolding question. Use the steps and examples to complete the answer to the question by writing the paragraphs on the scaffolding factors and linking them where possible. Alternatively you could use the grid to the right to structure your answer to the question. However, you could also use points of your own rather than the scaffolding factors.

INTRODUCTION
- Explain the key theme of the question.
- Suggest the key areas you are going to cover in your answer.

FIRST PARAGRAPH – FIRST SCAFFOLDING FACTOR (OR POINT OF YOUR OWN)
- Introduce the first factor.
- Fully explain this factor.
- Make a judgement about the importance of this factor.

SECOND PARAGRAPH – SECOND SCAFFOLDING FACTOR (OR POINT OF YOUR OWN)

THIRD PARAGRAPH – THIRD SCAFFOLDING FACTOR (OR POINT OF YOUR OWN)

FOURTH PARAGRAPH – FOURTH FACTOR
This could be an additional factor mentioned in the scaffolding or a point of your own.

CONCLUSION
- Begin with 'Overall ...'
- Make a final judgement on the relative importance of all the factors.

Examination practice

Example:
In the years 1928-39 Stalin introduced a series of Five-Year Plans that rapidly transformed Soviet industry. These Plans greatly changed the location and nature of Soviet industry. At the same time they transformed working and living conditions and encouraged the employment of women.

STEP 1 Write an introduction that identifies the key issues you need to cover in your answer and your main argument.

Example:
The first effect of the Five-Year Plans was to greatly change the role of women in the Soviet Union.

STEP 2 Introduce the first factor. This could be the factor mentioned in the question or a point of your own.

Example:
Women were encouraged to help in the Five-Year Plans and were now put on a more equal footing with men, able to gain jobs in all fields. Facilities such as crèches were provided to help them continue working after childbirth. Education for girls improved in order to provide the necessary skills to help with the development of industry. In 1929 the government reserved 20 per cent of places in higher education for women.

STEP 3 Fully explain the factor.

Example:
This was important because it raised the status of women and gave them more freedom. For example, they were able to obtain divorce on request and abortion was easily available.

STEP 4 Make a judgement on the importance of this factor.

Now have a go yourself at the next two factors. You may wish to add an additional factor mentioned in the scaffolding or one of your own.

Have a go yourself

Example:
Overall, the Five-Year Plans transformed Soviet industry in a short space of time. Each effect was of equal importance in different ways. Industrialisation brought major changes to the position of women and, in many cases, worsened the living and working conditions of the workforce. At the same time, it changed the face of industry, not only in scale but also location.

STEP 5 Write a conclusion making your final judgement on the question.

12 Life in the Soviet Union

> **Source A:** In 1934, Stalin announced in a speech that 'life was getting better'. Two years later the song 'Life's Getting Better' was written by Aleksandr Aleksandrov
>
> Beautiful as birds all in a row
> Songs fly above the Soviet land.
> The happy refrain of the cities and fields:
> 'Life's getting better
> And happier too!'
>
> The country is growing and singing as one,
> It forges everyone's joy with its songs.
> Look at the sun—the sun's brighter too!
> 'Life's getting better
> And happier too!'
>
> There's room everywhere for our minds and our hands,
> Wherever you go you'll find you have friends.
>
> Old age feels warmer, and youth braver still—
> 'Life's getting better
> And happier too!'
>
> Know, Voroshilov, we're all standing guard—
> We won't give the enemy even a yard.
> There is a saying for folks old and young:
> 'Life's getting better
> And happier too!'
> Let's let the whole gigantic country
> Shout to Stalin: 'Thank you, our man,
> Live long, prosper, never fall ill!'

Task

What image of life under Stalin is provided by the song in Source A? Pick out key words or phrases which provide this image.

Industrialisation, collectivisation and the **purges** brought rapid changes to the lives of people in the Soviet Union during the 1930s. The role of women, in particular, was transformed, although not necessarily for the better. Ethnic groups suffered more than most, especially from Stalin's policy of **Terror**, while living conditions for many worsened due to the demands of the Five-Year Plans.

This chapter answers the following questions:
- What were the experiences of different social groups?
- Did the position of women change?
- Why were ethnic groups persecuted?
- Did living conditions worsen under Stalin?

Examination skills
In this chapter you will be given the opportunity to practise some of the question types from Unit 2.

What were the experiences of different social groups?

Stalin's principal aim was to remove anyone considered to be a class enemy of socialism, especially **Nepmen**, *kulaks* and anyone who had capitalist tendencies. The **proletariat** was to rule supreme over the Soviet Union.

Party members

Stalin was determined to encourage peasants and members of the proletariat to become members of the Communist Party and rise to prominent positions. He wanted a career ladder for the new **elite** of the Party. By 1953, 50 per cent of this elite had risen from the ranks of the town and country **working class**, including later leaders such as Khrushchev and Brezhnev.

Moreover, the higher up the ladder you moved, the better your lifestyle. This could include better housing, better healthcare and even a villa, known as a *dacha*, for holidays in the countryside.

The peasants

Collectivisation and the purges removed the wealthier peasants, the *kulaks*. However, conditions for the mass of the peasantry were worse than those of town workers. The state kept prices low to ensure a cheap supply of food for the towns. As a result, more and more peasants moved to the towns to find work and, they hoped, a better standard of living.

The town workers

Stalin was also keen to encourage movement to higher positions in industry. Workers were promoted into management jobs in industry. For example, over 1.5 million workers gained management posts under the First Five-Year Plan. Some workers also benefited from the expansion of higher education which enabled them to gain the technical knowledge needed for higher management posts.

In addition, the rapid industrialisation caused by the Five-Year Plans removed unemployment completely. The down side was that the urban population rose from 29 million in 1929 to 40 million only four years later. This, in turn, led to poor living conditions. Furthermore, working conditions were harsh. Some peasants did not move to the towns because of the strict rules about discipline and punctuality as well as the productivity demanded as a result of the Stakhanovite movement (see page 108).

> **Source A:** From a speech by a brigadier (leader) of a collective farm made in 1938
>
> We have more than 600 hectares. Of those, 123 are sown with cotton, 225 planted with wheat. Our vineyards cover 45 hectares. Our three lorries can hardly cope with the work. Our farmers have built 70 new houses for themselves during the last years. Look inside these houses and you will find rich carpets and musical instruments. Four times this year the whole farm went to the theatre, to concerts and to the cinema. Look at our happy children. They all go to school. We have two schools. I could say much more about the life of our collective farm, but the young wine is bubbling impatiently in your glasses. Drink to the good Stalin, who brought us this life.

Source B: A painting by a Soviet artist in the mid-1930s. It shows the peasants on a collective farm celebrating the harvest

Tasks

1. What does Source A suggest about life for the peasants?

2. Source B was a propaganda poster. Devise a suitable caption that could have been used for this poster.

3. Who do you think was better off under Stalin, town workers or peasants? Give reasons for your answer.

4. *Describe the experiences of different social groups in the Soviet Union in the years 1928–41. (Remember how to answer this type of question? For further guidance, see page 39.)*

Chapter 12 Life in the Soviet Union

Did the position of women change?

Traditionally in Russia, and certainly before the Bolshevik Revolution of 1917, women were seen as second-class citizens with few rights. There were some changes under Lenin, with marriage and divorce made easy. Both parties simply had to agree and fill in a register. Abortion was made freely available on demand. There was greater equality for women in the workplace.

Family life

However, by the mid-1930s, the family was back in favour and divorce and abortion were less popular. The high divorce rate of the 1920s and early 1930s had created a great number of broken homes and homeless children who lived on the streets begging and robbing. Through propaganda, such as articles in Source A, the state tried to encourage families to stay together – for example, by:
- paying child allowances for married couples
- making divorce much harder
- restricting abortion.

Employment

Women continued to make progress in the area of employment. They were encouraged to work in almost all areas. Some women took on jobs like engineering, which had once been done only by men. However, life remained hard for most Soviet women. They were expected to work full time, as well as bring up a family. Help was provided by state nurseries and crèches.

> **Source A:** An extract from an article in *Pravda* in 1936
>
> *When we talk of strengthening the Soviet family we mean to fight against wrong attitudes towards marriage, women and children. 'Free love' and a disorderly sex life have nothing in common with Socialist principles or the normal behaviour of a Soviet citizen. The outstanding citizens of our country, the best of Soviet youth, are almost always devoted to their families.*

Political position

Politically, women still remained second-class citizens. Less than 20 per cent of the Communist Party was made up of women. Very few women rose to high positions in the Party or government.

> **Source B:** Government poster of the 1930s

The slogan reads 'The wide development of a network of crèches, kindergartens, canteens and laundries will ensure the participation of women in Socialist reconstruction'

Tasks

1. Study Source B. What message is the government trying to get across in this poster?

2. Draw a table like the one below and complete it using the information on women.

Progress	Lack of progress

3. Explain the effects of Stalin's government on the position of women in the Soviet Union in the years 1928-41. (Remember how to answer this type of question? For further guidance see page 60.)

Why were ethnic groups persecuted?

Although Stalin was from the non-Russian state of Georgia, he had no sympathy for the plight of the many non-Russian groups that had suffered **persecution** and '**Russification**' under the tsar. Indeed, they experienced a particularly difficult time in the 1930s. Stalin distrusted national groups which he believed might be disloyal to the regime. His aim was to turn these into 'Soviet citizens' rather than Ukrainians or Georgians. They were discouraged from speaking their own languages and practising their own customs and traditions. They were often discriminated against, with few having top positions in the army or government. Army recruits were sent away from their homelands and forced to mix with other ethnic groups.

Moreover, ethnic groups became one of the targets of Stalin's purges of the 1930s. From 1935 onwards, the Soviet government kept increasing 'cleansing' operations in border regions. Finnish, Latvian and Estonian families were deported from the Leningrad region to Kazakhstan and Siberia. At the same time families of Polish and German origin were deported from the border district of Kiev.

However, the largest deportations took place in 1936 when the entire Korean community, some 172,000 individuals, was moved from the Vladivostock and Birobidjan regions by the NKVD. It took 124 railway convoys to move them to Uzbekistan and Kakakhstan. This was justified on the grounds that the Korean population was 'a breeding ground for spies for the Japanese secret service'.

> **Source A:** From Maya Lykashtarnaya, whose father, Todar, was born in Belarus. He was arrested in 1937 and sent off to a labour camp, where he subsequently died
>
> *My mother hoped up to the very end, until they told her that he was sentenced to 10 years in jail without right of correspondence. This essentially meant that the person was no longer alive. This verdict was used when people were to be executed: sent away for 10 years, to some unspecified destination, without right of correspondence. My mother and myself also spent several years in a labour camp.*

> **Source B:** An interview with Roman Shin, whose Korean parents were forcibly deported in 1936.
>
> *These Korean people were deported without being asked anything, in cattle trains. My parents were also deported. People were sent to Kazakhstan, to the steppe, or to Uzbekistan. A number died on the way or when they arrived. Stalin claimed they were acting as spies for the government of Japan.*

Tasks

1. What does Source A suggest about the treatment of minorities in the Soviet Union?

2. Does Source B support the evidence of Source A about the treatment of ethnic minorities in the Soviet Union?

3. *Explain how ethnic minorities were treated in the Soviet Union in the years 1928-41.* (Remember how to answer this type of question? For further guidance, see page 84.)

Did living conditions worsen under Stalin?

There is much debate over the living conditions in towns and cities during industrialisation. There were some improvements but, for many, conditions were very poor.

Better conditions

No unemployment
Soviet workers did not experience an economic depression, unlike countries such as Britain, Germany and the USA where millions were out of work.

Family benefits
There were several benefits brought in for families. For example, there was a free health service for all, holidays with pay for many workers and an insurance scheme against accidents. In 1936 a new family law made divorce more difficult, while abortion became a criminal offence unless it was necessary on medical grounds.

Leisure
Sport and exercise were encouraged to improve the general fitness of Soviet men and women. Trade unions and collective farms provided clubs, sports facilities, film shows and general entertainment.

> **Source A:** Examples of activities in Moscow
>
> **Physical culture**
> *Sports stadium, training ground for acrobatics, volleyball, basketball and tennis, table games, wrestling and boxing rings and swimming school.*
> **Theatre**
> *Dramatic theatre – plays under the direction of H.P. Khmelev, visits to the Saratov Dramatic Theatre, children's music hall, cinema and newsreel theatre.*

Worse conditions

Overcrowding
As peasants flooded into towns and cities, pressure increased on all the basic amenities. Trams and buses were jam-packed. Flats had to be shared by several families. Often there was one family per room and they had to share the bathroom and kitchen. In Moscow only 6 per cent of households had more than one room.

> **Source B:** A painting showing Moscow in the mid-1930s

Family problems
Family structure was weakened. Wedding rings were abolished and abortion became available on demand. By 1934 there were 154,000 abortions, compared to only 57,000 live births. Marriages were carried out in brief ceremonies in registry offices. Divorce was easy and by 1934 there were 37 divorces for every 100 marriages.

Source C: A description of a Moscow apartment written in 1937

Badly built, with doors and windows of unseasoned wood, which would not shut properly, unpapered and thinly whitewashed walls, these rooms were home. By American and British standards we were living in a squalid tenement house. But by Russian standards we were housed almost like communist aristocrats.

Tasks

1. What does Source C suggest about living conditions?

2. Work in pairs. You are reporters who are interviewing two different families in Moscow in the mid-1930s, one that has benefited and one that has not. Write out your questions and answers.

Examination practice

Source A: From a history of Russia, published in 1996

Women were encouraged to work in new factories to ensure that the targets for the Five-Year Plans were reached. However, the number of deserted wives grew with the easing of the divorce laws. After 1936, divorce became harder to obtain and motherhood was encouraged. Medals were awarded to those mothers with large families.

1. What can you learn from Source A (above) about the role of women in the Soviet Union in the 1930s? (Remember how to answer this type of question? For further guidance, see page 24.)

2. Describe the key features of Stalin's policy towards the ethnic minorities in the 1930s. (Remember how to answer this type of question? For further guidance, see page 39.)

3. Explain the effects of Stalin's policies on different social groups. (Remember how to answer this type of question? For further guidance, see page 60.)

4. Explain why the position of women changed under Stalin. (Remember how to answer this type of question? For further guidance, see page 74.)

5. Explain how the lives of peasants and workers changed under Stalin in the years 1928–39. (Remember how to answer this type of question? For further guidance, see page 84.)

6. Was overcrowding in towns the worst effect of industrialisation in the Soviet Union in the years 1928–39?
You may use the following information to help you with your answer.
- Overcrowding in the towns
- Working conditions
- The Stakhanovite movement
- Slave labour

Chapter 12 Life in the Soviet Union

Revision activities

Key Topic 1: The collapse of the tsarist regime, 1917

1. Sketch four concentric circles. Then put the following effects of the First World War on Russia, in 1914–16, in rank order, beginning with the most important in the centre to the least important on the outside. Give a brief explanation of your choice of the most important:
   - Inflation
   - Influence of Rasputin
   - Food shortages
   - Military defeats

2. Each of the following lettered sentences should be paired with one of the numbered sentences on the right:
   (a) More and more peasants were called up to fight in the armed forces.
   (b) Russia suffered defeat after defeat during the first year of the war.
   (c) The tsar's frequent absences from Petrograd left the tsarina in charge of the government.
   (d) Russia did not have a transport system that could cope with the demands of war.
   (e) There were serious shortages of consumer goods such as boots and clothes.

   (i) She was greatly influenced by Rasputin.
   (ii) Vital supplies of food often failed to reach towns and cities.
   (iii) Therefore Tsar Nicholas II decided to take over the command of the armed forces.
   (iv) These shortages led to a rise in prices
   (v) This led to less land being ploughed and serious food shortages.

Key Topic 2: Bolshevik takeover and consolidation, 1917–24

1. Place the following events in chronological order:
   - Dissolution of the Constituent Assembly
   - Execution of the Tsar and his family
   - Red victory in the Civil War
   - Lenin's first decrees
   - Treaty of Brest-Litovsk

2. Explain why each of the following was important in the civil war in the years 1918–21:
   - Trotsky's train
   - Foreign support for the Whites
   - Admiral Kolchak
   - General Deniken
   - The *Cheka*

3. Make a copy of the following table. In less than five words for each column, summarise the differences between War Communism and the NEP:

	Why introduced	Key features	Successes	Failures
War Communism				
New Economic Policy				

4. Which of the following phrases best sums up the NEP?
   - It was an economic necessity but politically unpopular.
   - It was an economic necessity and politically unpopular.
   - It was a political necessity but economically unpopular.

   Explain your choice.

Key Topic 3: The nature of Stalin's dictatorship, 1924–39

1. What explanation can you give for the following contradictory statements?
   - Trotsky was the favourite to succeed Lenin and yet it was Stalin who became leader.
   - Lenin warned leading Bolsheviks against Stalin and yet Stalin became leader.

2. Make a copy of this table and match the following statements to either Trotsky or Stalin:

Strengths of Stalin	Weaknesses of Trotsky

   (a) He was too arrogant.
   (b) He had a key position as General Secretary of the Party.
   (c) He missed Lenin's funeral.
   (d) He was unpopular because he had been a Menshevik.
   (e) One problem was his Jewish background.
   (f) He was the chief mourner at Lenin's funeral.
   (g) He underestimated his chief opponent.
   (h) He promised 'Socialism in One Country'.
   (i) He wanted world revolution.
   (j) He placed supporters in leading positions in the Party.

3. Use illustrations to show the meanings of the following words and phrases:
   - The purges
   - Labour camps
   - Murder of Kirov
   - Show trials
   - Secret police

4. Which of the following are causes of and which are effects of the purges?

	Cause or effect?
The murder of Kirov	
The armed forces lacked leadership	
Millions were sent to labour camps	
Stalin's fear of the Old Bolsheviks	
Stalin had a persecution complex	
Slave labour was needed for industrialisation	
Stalin needed someone to blame for the failure of his policies	
All the Old Bolsheviks were eliminated	
Even the secret police were purged	

Revision activities

Key Topic 4: Economic and social changes, 1928–39

1. True or false?

	True?	False?
The First Five-Year Plan lasted four years		
The First Five-Year Plan concentrated on consumer goods		
Much industry was now located in the east		
The Third Five-Year Plan was interrupted by the German invasion of the Soviet Union		
Fines were introduced for lateness and absenteeism		
The Stakhanovites were popular with their fellow workers		

2. Match the following words to their definitions below:
   Stakhanovite, *Gosplan*, Magnitogorsk, shock brigades, *gulags*
   - State Planning Authority that set targets
   - Workers who exceeded their productivity targets
   - Groups of Stakhanovites
   - Labour camps
   - New industrial town

3. Make a copy of the following grid. In not more than ten words summarise the key change for each group.

	Key change
Women	
Ethnic minorities	
Peasants	
Workers	

4. The following account of life under Stalin is by a student who has not revised thoroughly enough. Rewrite the account, correcting any errors.

Fewer and fewer women worked in industry under Stalin. However, more and more women got top jobs in the Communist Party. At first divorce and abortion were difficult. Later, they were both made easier. Stalin supported the rights of the ethnic minorities because he was from the Ukraine.

Revision activities

Glossary

Abdicate To give up the throne.
All-Russian Congress of Soviets A meeting of representatives from the newly created soviets.
Allied Powers Britain, France and the USA.
Armaments Military equipment.
Autocracy Rule by one person who has complete power.
Autonomous Self-government.
Bolshevik A member of one of the groups formed after the split in the Social Democratic Party in 1903. The Bolsheviks (meaning 'majority'), led by Lenin, believed in a small party of dedicated revolutionaries.
Bolshevik Revolution This took place in October/November 1917 when the Bolsheviks seized power.
Budget deficit When a government spends more than it gets in revenue or taxes.
Buffer state A small country, often between two rival states.
Capitalism Economic system based on private ownership of the means of production, distribution and exchange.
Censorship Banning or cutting parts of a newspaper, book, film, etc., which the government does not like.
Civil rights The political, economic and social rights of a citizen, e.g. the right to vote and to be treated equally under the law.
Civil war War between people of the same country.
Collective farm A farm or group of farms managed and owned through the state.
Collectivisation Process introduced by Stalin whereby individuals' farms and land were put together and then run by a committee. All animals, tools and the produce of the farm were to be shared.
Comintern Short for 'Communist International' – international organisation based in Russia, formed to assist the growth of communism all over the world.
Commissar Term for government minister.
Commissar of Nationalities Minister or member of government responsible for non-Russians.
Commune A village organisation controlled by heads of families – it redistributed land and organised payment of taxes.
Constituent Assembly Parliament.
Constitution The system of rules by which a state is ruled.
Counter-revolution A revolution that tries to reverse the results of one that has just occurred.
Coup d'état Violent or illegal change of government.
Diplomatic isolation Many governments around the world refused to send ambassadors to the USSR and cut off all contact.
Elite An exclusive group or section.

Feudalism Medieval legal and social system in which people were obligated to their lord.
Five-Year Plan Set of targets for industry set by the central planning organisation, *Gosplan*.
Garrisoned (Of troops) stationed in a fortress or barracks.
Gosplan The State Planning Authority, which set targets for industries and allocated resources. An organisation run by the Communist Party. It was given the task of planning the industrialisation of the USSR under the Five-Year Plans.
*Gulag*s Prisons where inmates were punished by forced labour.
Haemophilia Hereditary disease that prevents the blood from clotting during bleeding. Even a minor cut could lead to excessive bleeding and death.
Hedonistic Indulging in sensual pleasures.
Ideology The ideas that characterise a political system.
Imports The purchase of goods or services from foreign countries.
Industrialisation Process of developing key industries, especially heavy industries such as coal and iron.
Inflation A rise in prices caused by too much money and credit, relative to the available goods.
Kremlin The twelfth-century citadel in the centre of Moscow containing the offices of the Soviet government.
Kulak The name given to the better-off peasants who had benefited from Lenin's New Economic Policy. By selling their produce, these peasants became better-off than other peasants and began to employ poorer peasants to work for them.
Land reform Changing methods of farming and assisting peasants with loans.
Liberal party A political party which follows ideas based on individual freedom and tolerance.
Marxism The thoughts of Karl Marx who was the founder of communism.
Menshevik A member of one of the groups formed after the split in the Social Democratic Party in 1903. The Mensheviks (meaning 'minority') believed the Party should be a mass organisation, which all workers could join.
Military dictatorship Rule by the armed forces.
Military Revolutionary Committee (MRC) A body originally set up by Social Revolutionaries and the Social Democrats to defend Russia against Germany and counter-revolution.
Mutiny Soldiers rebelling against their officers.
Nepmen Merchants/traders who became rich due to the New Economic Policy.

New Economic Policy Introduced in 1921 by Lenin to win back the support of the people. Allowed private businesses and farms and profit.

NKVD Name of secret police under Stalin.

OGPU The state security force which succeeded the *Cheka* (the Bolshevik secret police).

Old Bolsheviks Original Bolshevik Party members under Lenin.

Oratorical Public speaking.

Orthodox Church Branch of Christianity, strong in Eastern Europe, established by a breakaway from the Catholic Church in the early Middle Ages.

Persecution To mistreat an individual or group because of their race, class, political beliefs and/or religion.

Politburo The policy-making committee of the Communist Party in the Soviet Union.

Pravda The official Communist Party newspaper.

Proletariat The industrial working class.

Protector The ruler of Russia had influence in Eastern Europe and 'looked after' the interests of nationalities in this area.

Provisional Committee A temporary body set up until a permanent government could be established.

Provisional Government Temporary government set up after the abdication of Tsar Nicholas II.

Purge The systematic removal of enemies through terror.

Reactionary Someone totally opposed to reform.

Real wages The value of money earned in relation to the value of goods, i.e. what wages can buy.

Red Army The Soviet army.

Red Guard The Bolsheviks' own armed forces.

Requisitioning Seizing goods or produce.

Revolution A sudden and drastic change in a society's political, economic or cultural structures. Marx's view of a revolution was a violent overthrow of one system of production to the next – e.g. capitalism to socialism.

Right wing In this case, the less extreme communists who were prepared to accept some capitalist ideas.

Romanov dynasty Romanov was the family name of Tsar Nicholas. His family had ruled Russia since 1613.

Russification The policy of forcing non-Russians, such as Poles, to speak Russian and follow Russian customs.

Saboteur A person who deliberately destroys property.

Serf A person attached to the land and the property of the landowner.

Serfdom A system based on serfs working land that belongs to a landowner.

Shock brigades Groups of workers who were selected or volunteered for especially arduous tasks.

Show trials The trials of prominent politicians or opponents of the government, organised to demonstrate Stalin's power.

Social realism The official art form under Stalin, which was supposed to show the real life of peasants and workers but was used to glorify Stalin and his achievements.

Socialism The belief that all means of production should be owned and run by the government for the benefit of everyone and that wealth should be divided equally.

Socialist Believer in the idea that there should be state ownership and control of the means of production, distribution and exchange.

Socialist state A state in which everyone has an equal opportunity to benefit from the country's wealth, usually by having the main industries owned by the state.

Soviet An elected council of workers.

Spring Offensive The last major German attack on the Western Front in the First World War.

Stakhanovites Followers of Alexei Stakhanov (a miner, who, in the 1930s, had allegedly moved 102 tonnes of coal in one shift) who were dedicated to hard work.

Subsistence farming Producing just enough to live on with little or nothing left over to sell.

Supreme Soviet Soviets were local and regional workers' councils. Representatives from the regional soviets were sent to the Central or Supreme Soviet.

Terror Stalin's purges of the 1930s.

Testament Will.

Totalitarian state A state in which those in power control every aspect of people's lives.

Triple Entente Agreements made between Britain, France and Russia in 1907 in order to settle differences between them.

Utopian communist state A state where each citizen works freely for the sake of everyone else, using his/her own ability to the best advantage of society.

War Communism State control of industry and agriculture.

Working class Includes workers in industry, mainly in towns and cities.

World socialist revolution Lenin and Trotsky thought the Bolshevik Revolution would inspire workers all over the world to rebel against their governments and set up socialist states.

Answer to task 1, page 68: Lenin and Trotsky.

Answer to task 2, page 68: No.

Answer to task 2, page 75: Yezhov was purged by Stalin in 1938. This, in itself, is very strange as Yezhov was the Chief of the Secret Police responsible for carrying out many of Stalin's purges. After he was purged the picture was altered to remove him.

Index

1905 Revolution 14, 26, 32, 42
abortion 118, 120
agriculture 14, 62, 94
    farming methods 11, 95, 103
    grain crisis 1927 97
    mechanisation 98, 100, 102, 110
    modernisation 95, 96, 98
    New Economic Policy 65, 66, 97
    War Communism 61, 62–3
    see also collectivisation
Aleksandrov, Aleksandr 115
Alexandra, Tsarina 10, 15, 20, 22–3, 26
Alexei, Tsarevich 10, 15, 28
All-Russian Congress of Soviets 32, 42, 45
Alliluyev, Vladimir 79
Anastasia, Grand Duchess 58
April Theses 33, 42, 46, 50
aristocracy 12, 13
autocracy 8, 10, 14
Avdienko, A. 85, 86

banks 51
Battle of Tannenberg 19
Bloody Sunday 14
Bolshevik Revolution *see* October Revolution
Bolsheviks 16, 32, 70
    All-Russian Congress of Soviets 32, 42, 45
    July Days 34–5, 37, 42
    Kornilov Revolt 36–8, 42
    'Old Bolsheviks' 76, 78, 81
    party funds 42, 70
    party membership 33, 41, 42
    Petrograd Soviet 30
    Provisional Government 30
    securing control 50–3
    seizure of power 25, 41, 42–7, 49, 56
    soviets 33, 36, 50
    see also Communist Party
Buchanan, Meriel 17
Bukharin, Nikolai 71, 72, 73, 78, 81, 87, 96, 99

Cadets *see* Constitutional Democratic Party
capitalism 61, 65, 66, 67, 116
censorship 9, 14, 88
Central Committee 46, 72, 76, 92
changing history 75, 87
Cheka 51, 58, 64, 80
Chernov, Victor 52
civil war 49, 55, 56–9, 61, 62, 77, 96
collectivisation 85, 94, 95-104
    effects 102–3
    kolkhoz 100, 101, 104
    mechanisation 98, 100, 102
    opposition to 76, 104, 111
    sovkhoz 101
    see also agriculture
Communist Party 64, 66, 73, 82, 88, 92, 116, 118
    see also Bolsheviks

Congress of the Soviets of the USSR 86, 92
conscription 22, 58
Constituent Assembly 30, 36, 37, 38, 42, 47, 50, 56
    dissolution 52–3, 56
    Constitution of 1936 89, 92
Constitutional Democratic Party (Cadets) 16, 30, 51, 52, 56
consumer goods 65, 107, 110
Council of People's Commissars (*Sovnarkom*) 45, 50–1, 52, 54
Czech Legion 56, 57

Denikin, General 56, 58, 59
deportations 119
diplomatic isolation 96
divorce 51, 118, 120, 121
Dual Authority 30
dumas 14, 22, 23, 26, 27, 28, 29

education 14, 51, 90–1, 110, 116
elections 25, 47, 50, 52, 92
electrification of Russia 65
elite 16, 110, 116
ethnic groups 83, 115, 119
    see also national minorities

factories 110, 111
    First World War 22
    nationalisation 62
    ownership 62, 65, 67
    workers' control 51
    see also industrial production; industrialisation
family life 118, 120, 121
famine 11, 12, 13, 49, 56, 61, 63, 67, 102, 103
    see also food shortages
February Revolution 26–9, 32, 43
First World War 11, 17
    decision to continue 31, 32, 36
    defeats 19, 20–1, 25, 30, 31, 34, 37
    desertions 21, 30, 31, 37
    effects 22–3
    key military events 18-19
    Lenin's view 32, 33, 35, 46, 54
    peace 50, 54–5
Five-Year Plans 78, 85, 90, 94, 95, 96, 97, 98, 105, 106–12, 115
    First 76, 106-7, 110, 116
    results 108–10
    Second 107, 108
    targets 106, 107, 108, 110, 121
    Third 107
food seizures 62, 63, 97, 102
food shortages 22, 25, 26, 30, 56, 58, 62, 63, 67, 97, 98, 103
    see also famine
forced labour 78, 80, 105, 111
    see also gulags
foreign trade 65

Gapon, Father George 13, 14
German invasion 1941 82, 107
Ginsburg, Evgenia 81
Gosplan 106, 110
Greens, the 56, 58
Grey, Sybil 25
Guchkov, Alexander 16, 30, 32
gulags 64, 80, 88, 105, 111, 119
    see also forced labour

Hitler, Adolf 78, 82
housing 13, 110, 111, 120, 121

industrial production 11, 96, 106, 107, 108, 110
    armaments 78, 107
    First World War 20, 22
    New Economic Policy 65, 66, 67
    skill shortage 110
    see also Five-Year Plans
industrialisation 11, 14, 76, 79, 94, 96, 97, 105–12, 116
    peasants and 110, 111, 116
    women and 105, 110, 121
    see also factories; Five-Year Plans
inflation 22, 62
International Women's Day 27
Itskov, Iosti 69
Izvestiya 28, 42

July Days 34-5, 37, 38, 42

Kamenev, Lev 31, 34, 42, 71, 72, 73, 76, 81, 87
Kerensky, Alexander 16, 28, 30, 34, 35, 36, 37, 38, 42, 45, 47
KGB 82
Khrushchev, Nikita 112, 116
Kirov, Sergei 76, 78, 79, 80, 81
Kolchak, Admiral 56, 58, 59
kolkhoz 100, 101, 104
Komsomol 91, 109
Kornilov, Lavr 36–7
Kornilov Revolt 36–8, 42
Kravchenko, Victor 104
Kronstadt Mutiny 61, 64
Krymov, General 26
kulaks 66, 76, 98, 100, 104, 116

labour camps *see* forced labour; *gulags*
land 13, 16, 33, 62
    seizure 31, 35, 47, 50
League of the Godless 89
leisure 120
Lenin, Vladimir 16, 38, 49, 81, 83, 87
    April Theses 33, 42, 46, 50
    Constituent Assembly 52
    Council of People's Commissars 45
    death 66, 69, 71
    funeral 72, 73
    July Days 34–5, 42
    leadership of *Sovnarkom* 50–1

New Economic Policy 65–7
October Revolution 41, 42, 45, 46–7
opposition to First World War 32, 33, 35, 46, 54
return to Russia 31, 32, 46
slogans 35, 46
Treaty of Brest-Litovsk 54–5
Trotsky compared 44
War Communism 61, 62–3, 64, 99
Will and Testament 72
Lindhagen, C. 53
Lvov, Prince 30
Lykashtarnaya, Maya 119

Machine Tractor Stations (MTS) 100, 102
MacLean, Fitzroy 81
Mandelstam, Nadezhda 90
Mandelstam, Osip 82, 90
marriage 51, 118, 120
Martov, Julius 16, 43
Marx, Karl 16, 41, 46
Mensheviks 16, 30, 43, 45, 46, 52, 73
Michael, Grand Duke 26, 28
middle classes 12, 16, 23, 30
Military Revolutionary Committee (MRC) 43, 47
Milyukov, Paul 16, 30, 32
Mukhina, Vera 88

Narodniks 52
national minorities 8, 30, 56, 83, 119
 see also ethnic groups
Nechlyudov, Prince Dmitry Ivanovich 12
Nepmen 66, 67, 116
New Economic Policy (NEP) 61, 64, 65–7, 71, 72, 96, 97, 99, 106
newspapers 33, 34, 35, 36, 37, 42
 banning 50, 51
 censorship 9
 see also Izvestiya; Pravda
Nicholas II, Tsar
 abdication 25, 28, 29, 36
 death 58
 dumas 14, 22, 26, 27, 28
 February Revolution 26, 28
 First World War 20, 22
 opposition to 14–15
 rule 8–10
 weakness 10
NKVD 76, 77, 80, 82, 119

October Manifesto 14, 16
October Revolution 41–7, 64, 73, 87
Octobrists 15, 16, 30
Octobrists (youth group) 91
OGPU 80, 104
Okhrana 9, 26, 42
Olga, Grand Duchess 10
Orlov, Leonid 67
Orthodox Church 9, 89

peasants 30, 116
 Bolsheviks and 35
 civil war 58
 First World War 22
 industrialisation 110, 111, 116
 living conditions 11, 12–13
 move to towns 11, 13, 98, 102, 110, 111, 116, 120
 New Economic Policy 65, 67
 private trading 62, 65
 SRs and 16, 50
 War Communism 61, 62–3

 see also agriculture; collectivisation; land
Petrograd 22, 23, 33, 34, 37
 February Revolution 25, 26, 27, 28
 see also St Petersburg
Petrograd Soviet 28, 30, 31, 36, 37, 43, 44, 47
Pravda 34, 42, 52, 70, 86, 118
Prokofiev, Sergei 88
propaganda 75, 86, 88
Provisional Government 25, 28, 29, 41, 42, 43
 collapse 45, 49
 Kornilov Revolt 36–8
 reforms 32
 weaknesses and failures 30–5, 47
 purges 75–83, 115, 119

Rasputin, Gregory 15, 23, 26
Razannik, Ivanor 80
Red Army 56, 58, 59, 61, 62, 63, 64, 69, 73, 77, 98, 102
Red Guard 33, 34, 37, 38, 42, 43, 46, 52, 58
religion 9, 89
Rodzianko, Mikhail 15, 26, 27, 28
Russification 8, 83, 119
Ryutin, Martemyan 76

St Petersburg 14, 15, 23, 43
 see also Petrograd
Schapiro, Leonard 51
secret police 58, 77, 79, 80, 111
 Cheka 51, 64, 80
 jokes 77
 KGB 82
 NKVD 76, 77, 80, 82, 119
 OGPU 80, 104
 Okhrana 9, 26, 42
Serge, Victor 44, 62, 66, 88
Seventeenth Party Congress 76, 79
Shatunovskaya, Olga 79
Shin, Roman 119
shock brigades 108
Sholokov, Mikhail 104
Shostakovich, Dmitri 88
show trials 76, 81
Sissons, Edgar 53
Smolny Institute 43, 44, 45
Snow, C.P. 78
Social Democratic Party 16, 42, 43, 46
social realism 88
Socialism in One Country 72, 73
Socialist Revolutionaries (SRs) 16, 28, 30, 45, 46, 50, 52, 56, 59
Solzhenitsyn, Alexander 80
Sorokin, Pitirim 41
Soviet Order Number One 28, 30, 31
soviets 30, 50, 63, 64
 All-Russian Congress 32, 42, 45
 Bolsheviks and 33, 36
 Congress of the Soviets 86, 92
 Moscow 36, 56
 Petrograd 28, 30, 31, 36, 37, 43, 44, 47
sovkhoz 101
Sovnarkom see Council of People's Commissars
Stakhanov, Alexei 108
Stakhanovite movement 108, 116
Stalin, Joseph 31, 70
 Constitution of 1936 89, 92
 control of culture 88

 control of religion 89
 cult 75, 85, 86–7
 General Secretary of Communist Party 70, 72, 73
 October Revolution 45, 47, 71
 propaganda 75, 86, 88
 struggle for power 69–73
 Trotsky compared 69, 73
 see also collectivisation; industrialisation; purges
state control 62, 65, 94, 96, 99, 103, 106
State Planning Authority *see Gosplan*
Stolypin, Peter 14
strikes 9, 13, 14, 26, 27, 107
subject nationalities *see* national minorities
Supreme Council of National Economy 62
Supreme Soviet 92

Tauride Palace 30, 52, 53
Terror, the 82, 115
Tolstoy, Leo 9, 12
town workers 13, 14, 116
trade unions 9, 13
Treaty of Brest-Litovsk 54–5, 56, 71
Triple Entente 18
Trotsky, Leon 16, 38, 66, 76, 78, 81
 assassination 72, 77
 Bolsheviks 36
 February Revolution 29
 leadership of Red Army 58, 59, 64, 69, 71, 72, 73
 Lenin compared 44
 October Revolution 43–4, 45, 46, 47, 87
 Petrograd Soviet 37, 43, 44
 Stalin compared 69, 73
 struggle for power 71, 72, 73
 Treaty of Brest-Litovsk 54
tsarism 8–16, 26, 102
Tukhachevsky, Mikhail 77

unemployment 50, 116, 120
Union of Soviet Writers 88
Utley, Freda 111

Vesenkha 62
von Moltke, General 19

War Communism 58, 61, 62–3, 64, 99
Whites, the 56, 58, 59, 62, 63, 96
Winter Palace 14, 41, 44, 45, 87
Witte, Sergei 11
women 21, 41, 115, 118
 equality 50
 industrialisation and 105, 110, 121
Women's Battalion 45
Workers' Opposition 63, 64
working hours 13, 50

Yezhov, Nikolai 75, 77, 80
Young Pioneers 82, 91
youth groups 91
Yudenich, General 56, 58, 59
Yusupov, Prince 23

Zaleki, E. 107
Zinoviev, Gregory 42, 71, 72, 73, 76, 81, 87